THE ROAD TO
FORT SUMTER

THE

Thomas Y. Crowell Compan

New Yor

ROAD TO
FORT SUMTER

by LEROY HAYMAN

Illustrated by Louis S. Glanzman

FOR JOHN,

home from the wars

Contents

PROLOGUE ☆ End of the Road   *1*

ONE ☆ Cotton Empire   *13*

TWO ☆ Slave Life   *23*

THREE ☆ Slavery Under Law   *34*

FOUR ☆ Black Uprisings   *49*

FIVE ☆ White Advocates of Black
Freedom   *61*

SIX ☆ Douglass, Then Lincoln   *76*

SEVEN ☆ Two Compromises   *86*

EIGHT ☆ Kansas and Nebraska   *104*

NINE ☆ Polarization Proceeds   *115*

TEN ☆ John Brown and Dred Scott   *130*

ELEVEN ☆ The Debates, Then
Harpers Ferry   *143*

TWELVE ☆ Road to Sumter, Road to War   *155*

BIBLIOGRAPHY   *167*

INDEX   *169*

THE ROAD TO
FORT SUMTER

End of the Road

IT IS NOVEMBER OF 1860, and dark shadows are swiftly gathering over the land. Abraham Lincoln has just been elected President of the United States, but he is not the choice of a majority of the American voters. His total popular vote is a million shy of the combined total of his three opponents. This means that Lincoln is definitely a minority President-elect, who must soon try to govern a deeply divided land.

Why is the nation so deeply divided? Slavery, the holding of black people in bondage, is the basic issue. Slavery is legal in the Southern states; it is banned in the North. For decades it has been this way, but until now South and North have managed to get along. What has brought about the present rift?

One reason: the North wants slavery "contained" in the Southern states where it is now legal. The South wants slavery extended to the new territories in the West and Southwest that will eventually enter the Union as states. Unless slavery is allowed to expand, the slaveholding states will be hopelessly outvoted in Congress.

The South thus sees that the very institution of slavery itself is threatened. Many Southern families own slaves; many more would if they could afford to. Slaveholding is a form of wealth. Family fortunes, large or small, are invested in slaves, and family-owned plantations depend on slave labor. The whole Southern economy is based on slavery; the whole Southern way of life is geared to it.

With slavery challenged, many Southern states consider that they have no other course to take than to *secede*—to quit the Union and establish themselves as an independent nation. South Carolina, long the leader in asserting that slavery in the South must be preserved, is the first to go.

On December 17, a convention of 170 delegates from the state's electoral districts meet in Columbia, capital city of South Carolina. They gather in the

Baptist church, where the convention president, D. F. Jamison, says what they all want to hear: "As there is no common bond of sympathy or interest between the North and the South, all efforts to preserve this Union will be not only fruitless but fatal to the less numerous section [i.e., the South]." The delegates wildly applaud this statement.

Shifting to Charleston (to avoid a smallpox scare), they meet again to set secession into motion. On December 20 the Committee to Prepare an Ordinance of Secession presents a resolution:

We, the people of the State of South Carolina, do declare and ordain, and it is hereby declared and ordained, that the Ordinance adopted by us in Convention on the twenty-third day of May, in the year of our Lord one thousand seven hundred and eighty-eight, whereby the Constitution of the United States was ratified, and also all Acts and parts of Acts, of the General Assembly of this State, ratifying amendments of the said Constitution, are hereby repealed; and that the union now subsisting between South Carolina and other States, under the name of "The United States of America" is hereby dissolved.

The delegates vote unanimously for the resolution— and South Carolina is now out of the Union and on its own. Everyone in Charleston appears to be delighted with the break. Church bells peal; men march in parades; cannon are fired. This secession business seems simple enough.

But wait. What about the federal property and possessions located within the state? Aside from the usual post offices, lighthouses, and such, there are several forts and an arsenal in the Charleston area owned by the United States government. The arsenal is in the town proper. Out on Sullivan's Island, Fort Moultrie faces the sea, and is manned by a small party of United States soldiers. Tiny Castle Pinckney sits on a mud flat near the shore; it has one enlisted soldier as caretaker. Fort Johnson, a group of empty structures, is across the Ashley River, on James Island. And Fort Sumter, at the harbor entrance, is still being built. It has no occupants except the workmen who come out by boat every morning and return to shore each evening.

The secession convention takes it for granted that the forts are now the property of the state of South Carolina. All that is needed, the group believes, is for one of them to go to Washington, D.C., and arrange for the proper legal transfer of all the property once owned by the federal government.

But the new commander of Fort Moultrie has other ideas. He is Major Robert Anderson, a regular United States Army officer. He informs his superiors in Washington that he may have to take active steps to block a

Robert Anderson

takeover by South Carolina. The War Department in Washington warns him not to start hostilities, but also authorizes him "to take similar steps whenever you have tangible evidence of a design to proceed to a hostile act."

Anderson soon realizes that such "tangible evidence" is all about him and decides to move his troops from Fort Moultrie to the still unfinished Fort Sumter. Moultrie cannot really be well defended, Anderson judges; Sumter will be a better base for armed action. On December 26 he gives the order to transfer guns, ammunition, supplies, and personnel. The South Carolina guard vessel almost stops his boats in the fog, but the guard is unable to see anything amiss. The federal boats proceed to Sumter at the mouth of the harbor without incident.

Immensely relieved, Major Anderson, a devoutly religious man, writes his wife: "Thanks be to God. I give them with my whole heart for His having given me the will and shewn the way to bring my command to this Fort. I can now breathe freely. The whole force of S. Carolina would not venture to attack us. . . . Praise be to God for His merciful kindness to us. I think that the whole country north and South should thank Him for this step."

President James Buchanan, now in the waning months of his administration, realizes that Sumter must be strengthened. He authorizes plans to send the U.S.S. *Brooklyn*, a navy steam sloop, with men and munitions to the fort. Thinking the plan over, Winfield Scott, the commanding general of the United States Army, decides that a merchant vessel has a better chance of sneaking undetected into the harbor at Charleston with its cargo.

On January 5, 1861, he dispatches the *Star of the West*, a side-wheel merchant steamer, on its way to Charleston from New York. Aboard are 250 troops, as well as food and ammunition. Early on the morning of January 8, the *Star of the West* enters the harbor and tries to approach Sumter.

But a hail of shells from South Carolina batteries crosses the bow of the unarmed *Star of the West*; indeed, one missile smashes into its side. The ship is forced to turn back to sea. Meanwhile Major Anderson is faced with a terrible decision. Should he fire back in defense of the *Star of the West*? If he does, he knows that war will break out between the United States and South Carolina. Anderson decides to hold his fire.

Instead he writes to South Carolina's Governor Pickens:

Two of your batteries fired this morning upon an unarmed vessel bearing the flag of my government. As I have not been notified that war has been declared by South Carolina against the government of the United States, I cannot but think that this hostile act was committed without your sanction or authority. Under that hope, and that alone, did I refrain from opening fire upon your batteries.

Further, Anderson demands a direct statement of disavowal of belligerent intent. Otherwise, he says, he will consider the firing an act of war and thereafter will not "permit any vessels to pass within range of the guns of my fort."

Governor Pickens replies at once. He asserts that the United States is "imposing upon this State [South Carolina] the condition of a conquered province" and that the firing was justified. A few days later he strongly urges Major Anderson to surrender Sumter to South Carolina—"to prevent bloodshed."

For a time, however, Fort Sumter is not threatened. Anderson uses this period to strengthen the fortifications and deploy his weapons. But after the incident over the *Star of the West*, Washington does not care to attempt to reinforce Sumter further for the present. The War Department is playing a waiting game, unable to see into even the immediate future.

During the interval six other Southern states secede and form the Confederate States of America. Governor Pickens demands that his South Carolina forces be allowed to seize Sumter because it stands as a symbol of United States authority over his state. But Jefferson Davis, newly elected president of the Confederacy, restrains him. Telling him in effect to calm down, he assures Pickens that action will soon be taken, not by South Carolina alone, but by a united South.

In March President Davis sends Pierre Gustave Toutant Beauregard, a brigadier general in the Confederate army, to be military commander of Charleston. Beauregard at once revamps the plans for the capture of Sumter. The new plans concentrate on keeping federal reinforcements from coming to the aid of Sumter, rather than making a direct attack on the fort itself. Major Anderson warns the War Department that only a strong fleet can now reach the fort.

Lincoln is inaugurated as sixteenth President of the United States on March 4, and the rumors begin. Will Sumter be evacuated? Will Sumter be defended? Anderson's food supplies are running low. Sooner or later, some action must be taken, but day after day slips by. Plans are made, then changed, finally canceled. For the moment nothing happens. March ends; April begins.

Finally on April 8 a War Department clerk named Robert Chew appears in Charleston with a note of instructions from President Lincoln that says:

You will proceed directly to Charleston, South Carolina; and if, on your arrival there, the flag of the United States shall be flying over Fort Sumpter, and the Fort shall not have been attacked, you will procure an interview with Gov. Pickens, and read to him as follows: "I am directed by the President of the United States to notify you to expect an attempt will be made to supply Fort Sumpter with provisions only; and that, if such attempt be not resisted, no effort to throw in men, arms or ammunition will be made without further notice. . . ."

Governor Pickens immediately forwards the message to the headquarters of the Confederate government in Montgomery, Alabama, asking for instructions. The answer comes back, clear and concise: the continued occupation of Fort Sumter by federal troops can no longer be tolerated. Anderson and his men must go.

On April 11 Beauregard demands that Anderson surrender the fort at once. Anderson refuses, but confesses that he will soon be starved out. How soon? Beauregard's representative insists on knowing. By April 15, Anderson answers—unless the United States government sends food or makes other arrangements.

The answer does not satisfy Beauregard's aides, who announce that Confederate guns will start firing on Fort Sumter.

At four thirty on the morning of April 12, 1861, the first shot of the Civil War is fired. A Confederate cannonball from a gun at Fort Johnson, on James Island, bursts over Sumter. For thirty hours Anderson's troops trade shells with Confederate batteries which ring the harbor. But the Union men are outgunned, and their food is virtually gone.

On April 13 Anderson is forced to surrender the fort. He and his ninety men evacuate Sumter and go aboard the steamer *Ysabel* bound for New York. The Union men march out to drumbeats, tired but very angry.

The road to Sumter has come to an end. But the end is also a beginning: the beginning of the bloody war of brother against brother that will last for four years —almost to the day—and desolate the South. It will bring an end to legal slavery for the blacks but only the start of their search for true freedom.

Where did this road to Sumter begin? No map traces its course. It began in a time, rather than in a place, a time when the United States of America was itself beginning.

Cotton Empire

"I WONDER, I wonder, I wonder . . . ?"

Questions coursed through Eli Whitney's mind as he watched. Seated on rough wooden benches in a low open shed, black slaves were picking green seeds from the tufty bolls of raw cotton. Working as fast as they were able, none of them could clean more than a few pounds of cotton a day. The seeds clung to the staples, or fibers, of the cotton; they were hard to pull free.

Yet cotton mills in the northern United States were ready to roll if they could get large supplies of seed-free cotton. Mills in England were even more eager for the stuff. Cotton fabrics, already being turned out in small quantities, were proving popular. Unlike wool, cotton could be washed. Unlike linen, cotton fabric could be inexpensively produced. But wool and linen were the only domestic fibers used for fabrics until cotton came along.

Yet if removing the seeds proved so difficult, how could the few cotton planters in the American South begin to meet the demand? They were about ready to give up. They were about ready to admit that short-staple green-seeded cotton couldn't be cleaned and turned over to the mills at a low price—a price that would allow cotton to compete with such fibers as wool and flax (from which linen is made).

Wool and flax didn't require the picky kind of cleaning that raw cotton did. This cleaning was expensive, even though the slaves who did the work drew no pay. After all, slaves—or their parents or grandparents—must be purchased. They must somehow be fed and clothed and nursed when sick. All this took money. Thus slaves had to earn their keep. That was the way the slave system in the southern United States worked.

Then Eli Whitney, a Yankee from Massachusetts making his first visit to the South in 1792, began to wonder.

Eli Whitney had already done a lot of wondering in his young lifetime. Born in 1765, he was now twenty-seven years old. He was a New Englander, reared on a farm in Worcester County, Massachusetts, about forty miles west of Boston. As a small boy he had wondered how things worked. His older sister Elizabeth later wrote:

Our Father had a workshop and sometimes made wheels of different discriptions [sic]. He had a lathe to turn chairposts and quite a variety of tools. This gave my Brother an opportunity of learning the ways of tools very young. He lost no time, as soon as he could handle tools he was always making something in the shop and seemed not to relish working on the farm.

As a teen-ager during the American Revolution, Eli went into business for himself. He forged nails for the government and for private purchasers, and he did so well that he hired an assistant. But the end of the war and the new competition from the old enemy—Great Britain—washed young Whitney out of business. Not until he was eighteen or so did he even think about going to college. Then he set about to prepare himself with the proper background—mainly Latin and Greek —and to earn some money for his college expenses.

Yale was his college, and most of his classmates were studying to be ministers or lawyers. Nevertheless,

Whitney found much at Yale to satisfy his scientific, problem-solving mind.

The college had a room over the chapel in which it housed its science equipment, or "philosophical apparatus," and Whitney spent long hours there. In "the museum," there was a telescope, a micrometer, an orrery (a contraption that demonstrated the motion of the planets), as well as many devices that illustrated physical principles. For the late eighteenth century it was an impressive array of scientific gear. And it helped to answer Whitney's many questions about how things worked.

Whitney was years older than his fellow students when he was graduated. At once he was hired as a tutor to the children of a Major Dupont of South Carolina. For company's sake he traveled south with the family of Mrs. Catherine Greene, widow of the Revolutionary War commander, General Nathanael Greene.

The Greene plantation, called Mulberry Grove, was in Georgia, a long way from New England. Mrs. Greene, like most of her prosperous neighbors, owned slaves. The first national census, taken just two years before Whitney's journey south, put the total population of the United States at nearly four million. Of these, more than three quarters of a million were blacks, and most of them were slaves. And nearly 90 per cent of the slaves were owned by Southern masters.

But this did not mean that all Southerners owned slaves. Indeed, by 1860, the last census to give slave statistics, there were about 8,000,000 white people in the South and only 384,884 of them owned blacks. More than 200,000 owners held five or fewer slaves. There were many whites in the towns and on the small farms who owned no slaves at all. Thus slavery was not a universal practice in the South—but where it existed, plantation owners claimed they could not get along without it.

Whitney intended to stay only a few days at the Mulberry Grove plantation, then go on to the Dupont place in South Carolina. He never got there.

Instead he saw the slaves picking the green seeds out of the cotton, seed by seed. And he began to wonder. Somewhere in his restless search for factual information, he had already picked up the knowledge that another variety of cotton—with black seeds and long staples, or fibers—was being grown in Sea Island, Georgia, and a few other locations. He knew too that a machine called a *rolling gin* ("gin" being short for *engine*) was used to comb the seeds out of this variety and to make it ready for the mill. But the long-staple cotton fibers were fairly smooth. They did not bunch and knot around the black seeds as the short-staple cotton fibers did around their green seeds.

Whitney realized that the simple comb idea in the rolling gin would not work for short-staple cotton. Another principle, another machine, were needed. In ten days at Mulberry Grove he fashioned a working model of a machine to remove the green seeds from short-staple cotton. It was simple in design, but it did the job. This new cotton gin, unlike the rolling gin, had wire teeth on opposing rollers. The teeth meshed as the raw cotton was fed between the rollers, and the meshed teeth combed out the seeds.

"I made [a machine] . . . ," Whitney later wrote his father, "which required the labour of one man to turn it and with which one man will clean ten times as much cotton as he can in any other way before known and also clean it much better than in the usual mode. This machine may be turned by water or with a horse, with the greatest ease. . . . It makes the labour fifty times less, without throwing any class of People out of business."

Instead the simple cotton gin put one "class of People" into business. It put the plantation owners into the cotton-growing business on a lavish scale. It made them suppliers of raw cotton to the soon-to-be-booming cotton mills of New England and old England.

The cotton gin did more. It made slavery—Negro slavery, black slavery—into a profitable enterprise. It made the black slave into a far more valuable piece of property. And it deepened a controversy and a conflict that was settled legally (but not emotionally and spiritually) by the North's triumph in the Civil War and by the Thirteenth, Fourteenth, and Fifteenth amendments to the United States Constitution that were passed after that war.

Before the cotton gin was invented, it looked for a brief period as though slavery—and the whole plantation system—was becoming economically unsound. In the early 1790's the principal Southern cash crops were rice, tobacco, and indigo (for making blue-black dyes). But the demand for these crops was diminishing in the markets of the world. One of the crops, tobacco, exhausted the soil after a few plantings, and the tobacco grower had to find new land on which to raise his crop. Thus the South was in the grip of an economic depression. It was desperately seeking to cut back or to find another way to survive.

Under these conditions the black slave was an economic hazard. It cost some owners more than their slaves produced to furnish them with food, clothing, and a place to sleep. For a little time, then, many slave-owners were thinking about setting their slaves free. The owner would lose the money he had invested in his black, but he would no longer have to support this piece of human property.

Then Eli Whitney's cotton gin made cotton a profitable crop and transformed a depressed South into a prospering land.

Whitney had no notion of what he had done to the slave, nor did he have any intention of doing it. Nevertheless, his cotton gin tightened the hold of slavery on the South. The Yankee inventor made slavery a sound investment.

Thus from a few bales of cotton raised mainly for experiment before the 1790's, production rose to more than 160 million pounds by 1820, doubled that by 1830, more than a billion pounds by 1850, and an astounding 23 billion pounds by 1860. In that year cotton amounted to about two thirds of all United States exports.

Cotton became big business, an agricultural empire. It brought the South into the Industrial Revolution that was already sweeping western Europe and the

northern United States. But that empire depended on the enslavement of human beings who differed from their masters only in the color of their skins.

Slavery, which had shown signs of faltering, was now strong. The road to Sumter really begins with the entrenchment of this "peculiar institution" in the South.

Slave Life

WHAT WAS it like to be a slave? What kind of life did a slave lead?

Some slaves had been born in freedom in their native Africa. They lived mainly in the savanna or the tropical rain forest of West Africa, growing up in the ways of their own tribe, their own people. They were deeply involved in family life and religion. And they lived in a complex web of tradition, culture, and custom, a civilization that was very different from that of the white man. In its own way, however, the black civilization was just as developed and as satisfying.

The blacks of West Africa had a glorious history to look back upon. In ancient days the kingdoms of

Ghana (from which the nearby modern republic takes its name), Mali, and Songhai had had powerful rulers, proud cities, and busy markets. There they had courts of law, schools for the young, and an extensive social life. In the seventeenth century and early years of the eighteenth century, however, these advanced civilizations had suffered a decline, and a kind of Dark Ages had set in. About the same time the earliest European explorers and traders began to arrive.

It was an evil day when Muslim raiders or black chiefs from enemy tribes came on slave-raiding expeditions. The West Africans put up a stubborn resistance, and the slaughter was sickening. But in the end many men and women, adults and children, were captured and shackled. They were brought to ports on the Atlantic coast of Africa and sold to European or American captains of slave ships anchored in the harbor.

Then began the long journey, six weeks or more, across the ocean to the West Indies or to American coastal cities. For the captive blacks, the trip was a hellish nightmare.

Hundreds of blacks were forced into the ship's small holds, crowded so close that there was no room to lie down. They were chained in place and fed only bits of rotten food and sips of brackish water. One black out of every four or five did not survive the voyage; the dead and the dying were thrown overboard. Some went mad; and some, mad or sane, committed suicide.

The United States Constitution provided that Congress could pass a law banning the importation of slaves after 1808; this had been done, but the law was freely flouted. As long as slavery was profitable, there were slave ships bringing their cargoes of human misery to American ports. As late as 1859–60, a year or so before the start of the Civil War, at least a hundred slave ships sailed out of New York Harbor on their grim missions. And this despite the fact that New York State had officially abolished slavery sixty-five years before.

Olaudah Equiano was one African-born slave who lived to tell his story. Captured as a young boy from his village in West Africa, he was transported to the West Indies. There he became a slave sailor and also, by one means or another, picked up an education. One of his captains renamed him Gustavus Vasa, after the sixteenth-century Swedish king. Here is how he later described the agony of his first voyage across the Atlantic:

. . . now that the whole ship's cargo [of slaves] were confined together, [the hold] became absolutely pestilential. The closeness of the place and the heat of the climate, added to the number in the ship, which was so crowded that each had scarcely room to turn himself, almost suffocated us. This produced copious perspirations, so that the air soon became unfit for respiration, from a variety of loathsome smells, and brought on a sickness among the slaves, of which many died. . . . This wretched situation was again aggravated by the galling of the chains, now become unsupportable; and by the filth of the necessary tubs, into which the children often fell and were almost suffocated. The shrieks of the women and the groans of the dying rendered the whole a scene of horror almost inconceivable.

Sometimes buyers came aboard ship to purchase slaves. Once on land the remaining slaves were hustled off to a market where they were auctioned off. The slave being bid for was stood on a block and stripped nearly naked, and prospective buyers closely examined his muscles, his eyes, his teeth. If the black had already served under a master in the United States, his back was examined for scars of beating. A scarred slave was a rebellious slave, one to be avoided.

If a black husband and wife had managed to stay together on the long ocean voyage, they were often sold to separate buyers, never to see each other again.

In the same way children were sold away from their parents; and family ties—so important in African tribal life—were forever destroyed.

Uprooted from their culture and language, torn away from their families and tribes, their history and religion, the slaves tended to lose their whole African tradition and heritage. They were never taught English, but picked it up by ear, forgetting most of their African tongue in the process. The result was a kind of "pidgin English" by which they could understand one another well enough, but which outsiders found hard to fathom.

On a large plantation a slave was either a house servant or a field hand. As house servant, the black cooked the meals, waited on table, served as a butler or valet (if a man), as a maid or attendant (if a woman). The slaves did all the housework. They tended the flowers and shrubs and the rolling lawns. From infancy the children of the white master were cared for by black nursemaids. Often there was a deep bond of affection between the white child and his black nurse. As the child grew, however, he learned that his society took for granted the services and loyalty of black people.

The house servants ate in the kitchen and had the

run of the place. Some even had sleeping quarters in the house itself; but most of the blacks—house servants and field hands alike—slept in the slave quarters located a little distance from the master's mansion.

Despite the fact that servants and field hands shared the same quarters, a marked social distinction was made between them. Because the servants lived on such close terms with the master's family, eating the same food, often wearing the white family's cast-off garments, they tended to think of themselves as superior to the field workers. They knew most of the family's "secrets," were familiar with the family's friends, and sometimes imitated the family's habits and mannerisms.

Life was far different for the field hands. They worked a back-breaking long day, fourteen or fifteen hours. They plowed, planted, cultivated, and harvested, cared for the livestock, and did the thousand and one chores needed to keep a plantation going. Their workday began before dawn and ended long after dark. As night fell, the exhausted field hands trooped home to their little windowless cabins chinked with plaster or mud. Only then did they have time to cook their main meal of the day. They lit a fire, broiled slices of bacon over the coals, and in the ashes baked cakes made of ground corn meal mixed with water. They ate their simple supper with their fingers, sometimes using a large, flat chip of wood as a plate.

The women worked as hard as the men and at the same tasks. Their small children were tended by a black grandmother too old to work in the fields. When a child reached the age of six or so, he went to work— on easy chores at first, but soon the same strenuous labor as his parents. No schooling was permitted, and only a very few blacks learned to read and write.

Young girl slaves were encouraged to marry—or to live with a black man—and have many children. Many slaveowners rewarded their black mothers for each new baby. Every small child was worth money to its owner, and its value increased as the child grew tall and strong.

On most plantations each slave was given a regular clothing allowance. A man might get two cotton shirts, a pair of woolen pants, and a woolen jacket in the fall; in the spring, two cotton shirts and two pairs of cotton trousers. A woman might be allotted, spring and fall, cotton and woolen cloth for dresses and a supply of thread and buttons. Each person would get one pair of shoes a year and a blanket every second or third year. Shoes came in only two sizes—large and small. Socks and stockings were unheard of.

If a slave had a special skill he might be hired out. A

trained carpenter or blacksmith might earn several dollars a week for his master. This practice went on mainly in Southern towns and cities. Some slaveowning families, in fact, got their whole income from renting out their slaves. As a slave he was only a piece of property, with no legal claim on the fruits of his labor.

On larger plantations, with twenty or more slaves, the master rarely had direct contact with his field hands. Instead, an overseer, usually a white man, would be in charge. Often the overseer was a true slave driver. With his loud voice, his bullying ways, and his big blacksnake whip, he would drive the slaves to the limits of their strength. He ruled by fear and the lash, and the slaves usually hated him far more than they did their master. These field hands saw their master only from a distance—but the overseer loomed large and savage directly over them.

The master and his family sometimes came to the slave quarters on a Sunday morning and sat with the blacks as a Negro preacher conducted a religious service. For the most part, the preacher was a slave too, a man who worked six days a week in the fields alongside the others.

The blacks adopted the suffering Christ as their own. To them Jesus became the symbol of their own plight and misery. And some of the black preacher's African heritage crept into his sermons and into the music of the hymns.

The influence of African musical forms on the old Protestant hymns soon produced a new kind of music —the Negro spiritual. The music and perhaps some of the ideas behind the words were from Africa. But the words themselves were English, and the images were drawn from the Protestant Old and New Testaments.

Sometimes the lyrics to a hymn achieved a true poetry:

I'd a like to die as a Jesus die,
And he die wid a freely good will,
He lay in de grabe, an' he stretchy out his arms,
O Lord, remember me.

The slaves were kept hard at work six days a week and often on the seventh if plantation tasks, such as harvest, demanded it. But on many plantations the week between Christmas and New Year's Day was set aside as a kind of vacation for the blacks. The farmwork was done, and the slaves were free to gather and inject a little cheer into their drab lives. They gambled with the pennies scraped together and hoarded all year long. They drank the home-distilled whiskey usually forbidden them. They danced to the music of home-made banjos and fiddles. They sang their spirituals and "shouts" and lively work songs. And they tried for a little while to forget the hopelessness and despair and emptiness of their enslaved existence.

Slavery Under Law

HOW WERE blacks from Africa first brought to America? The first Negroes came to the New World by way of Europe. Muslim traders had transported slaves from Africa and sold them in western Europe for many centuries. But it was not until the fifteenth century that the Europeans themselves began bringing in blacks.

In the fifteenth century Prince Henry the Navigator of Portugal began sending ships down the west coast of Africa, searching for a way around the continent and on to the fabled wealth of Asia. During their voyages south and north, Henry's captains purchased blacks in chains and brought them back to serve Portuguese noblemen. Soon wealthy Spaniards and Frenchmen were also buying slaves.

Some historians claim that Pedro Alonso Niño, who sailed with Columbus, was black. True or not, there were Negroes who came to the New World with the first Spanish explorers and conquistadores. Thirty free blacks accompanied Balboa as he crossed the Isthmus of Panama to find the Pacific Ocean. Negroes aided Cortés in his conquest of Mexico and helped Pizarro become the short-lived master of Peru. They were with Coronado as he searched the southwest for the mythical Seven Cities of Cibola. Blacks were in virtually every Spanish and Portuguese expedition that probed the two American continents.

But the first slaves in the Americas, especially in South America, were not black. They were Indian, the people who were living on the land when the New World was discovered by Europeans. Columbus enslaved the Arawak Indians for his West Indies colonies. And when the Portuguese launched their vast sugar plantations in Brazil early in the sixteenth century, they captured the Indians and put them to work.

The Indians, however, proved poor slaves. Indian men were hunters and warriors, accustomed to roaming at will. Forced to hard labor in the fields, many sickened and died. Others waited only for a chance to escape. The Spanish and Portuguese planters in Latin

America soon began to import black slaves from Africa. They were more used to living in communities than the Indians were, and already accustomed to farm work. Another advantage: blacks were better able to withstand the diseases of the Europeans. Among the Indians, the common cold (a European-fostered illness) became a raging and deadly epidemic.

The first blacks reached North America in 1619. English colonists at Jamestown, Virginia, bought twenty of them from a Dutch trading vessel that moored in the harbor. These Negroes were not slaves, but bondsmen. It was an important distinction. As a bondsman, or bond servant, a person was "bonded" to his owner for only a set number of years. At the end of that time he was free and his own man.

Many native Englishmen came to America as bondsmen. For assuming the obligations of a bondsman, a person's debts in England were settled and his passage paid to the New World. But many white bondsmen in Virginia were soon in the habit of slipping free of their bonds before their time was up. They would melt into the wilderness or find their way to another settlement and pass themselves off as free men.

The black bondsmen could not do this. The color of their skins would mark them in a strange place as runaways. From the very beginning they were treated differently from white bondsmen, and in 1682 English law made all blacks in America into slaves. Their legal rights were taken away, and their chances for freedom in their own lifetime irrevocably lost.

At the start of the eighteenth century there were perhaps ten or twelve thousand slaves in the Virginia colony, with another thousand or so brought in each year from Africa. These new arrivals and the growing slave families had swelled the number of blacks in Virginia to well over two hundred thousand by the start of the American Revolution in 1775. At that time there were about five hundred thousand blacks in the colonies altogether.

In many areas the number of blacks was increasing much faster than the number of whites. In some places blacks actually outnumbered whites—there were, for example, about ninety thousand Negroes in the Carolinas in 1765, and only forty thousand white people. Towns were small in those days, and virtually all slaves worked on the mixed-crop farms and plantations. The white masters knew the value of their blacks and kept encouraging them to breed and multiply. And the masters continued to buy more blacks at the coastal slave marts. There traders auctioned off the new im-

ports delivered by the slave ships or the "civilized" blacks owned by men who wished to turn their slave holdings into cash.

Thus the South became more and more deeply involved in slavery. At the same time, however, the masters were becoming frightened of what they had created—a force that could suddenly expand to explosive dimensions. Soon they began passing laws that shackled the slaves as effectively as chains would have done. In 1686 the South Carolina colonial legislature voted to prohibit a slave's leaving his master's property between sundown and sunup, unless he had a written note from his owner. For stealing a hog or a chicken he was to be branded on the cheek.

As the number of slaves in the Southern colonies increased, the penalties for even petty offenses grew harsher. The Southern slaveowners were learning to rule by fear and force.

In the New England colonies it was a somewhat different story. At the start of the American Revolution there were no more than twenty thousand blacks in all of New England, and some of these had already won or bought their freedom by one means or another. The total white population of New England during this period was close to seven hundred thousand.

The huge Southern plantations, where slave labor was used, produced one main crop—before cotton, it was rice, tobacco, or indigo. There were plenty of smaller farms in the South, but these grew a variety of subsistence crops that were mainly consumed right at home. Most of the New England farms were like these smaller Southern farms—and neither of them used slaves.

Those New England farmers who owned blacks had only a few, and the owner worked in the fields alongside his slaves. In the New England communities, blacks acted as messengers, porters, even clerks. They had to be allowed some freedom of movement to carry out their duties. Indeed, many were taught to read and to write because their jobs required such skills.

There may have been few slaves in New England itself, but many merchants in Boston, Salem, and other seacoast towns were deeply involved in the slave trade. The prime business of these merchants was rum manufactured from West Indies sugar. How to pay for the sugar? Why, with slaves imported from West Africa. And how to pay for the slaves? Why, with rum manufactured in New England. This three-way operation was known as "the triangular trade," and the shrewd merchants, owning their own slave ships as well as the rum distilleries, grew immensely wealthy.

Yet many New Englanders early began to think that slavery should be abolished. In part their belief arose because there were so few blacks in the area. Slave labor was not necessary to the farms and businesses of New England. In part this feeling came from a genuine dislike of the idea that a human being could be enslaved, made to serve a master by force and without choice.

For their part, the Negroes of Massachusetts were soon agitating for freedom. Their petition to the Massachusetts House of Representatives in 1777 began with these words:

The petition of a great number of blacks detained in a state of slavery in the bowels of a free and Christian country humbly shows that your petitioners apprehend that they have in common with all other men a natural and unalienable right to that freedom which the Great Parent of the universe has bestowed equally on all mankind and which they have never forfeited by any compact or agreement whatever. But they were unjustly dragged by the hand of cruel power from their dearest friends and some of them even torn from the embraces of their tender parents, from a populous, pleasant, and plentiful country and in violation of the laws of nature and of nations, and in defiance of all the tender feelings of humanity, brought here . . . to be sold like beasts of burden and like them, condemned to slavery for life. . . .

By the time the Revolution started, there was a mounting sentiment against slavery in New England. The South, however, had built its plantation economy around slavery, and it resented New England's pious diatribes against the practice. After all, New England had little to lose by the abolition of slavery. But a ban on slavery would impoverish the South.

Thomas Jefferson, himself a Virginia slaveowner (and sometimes ashamed of the fact), was made sharply aware of the Southern attitude. In June 1776 the Continental Congress chose Jefferson to prepare a draft of what was to become the Declaration of Independence. Much of that famous document consists of charges against Britain's king, George III. In the first draft Jefferson wrote:

He [King George] has waged cruel war against human nature itself, violating its most sacred rights of life & liberty in the persons of a distant people who never offended him, captivating and carrying them into slavery in another hemisphere, or to incur miserable death in their transportation thither. . . . Determined to keep open a market where MEN should be bought and sold, he has prostituted his negative [i.e., veto] for suppressing every legislative attempt to prohibit or to restrain this execrable commerce; and that this assemblage of horrors might want no fact of distinguished die, he is now exciting these very people to rise in arms among us, and to purchase that liberty of which he deprived them, by murdering the people upon whom *he* also obtruded them; thus paying off former crimes committed against the *liberties* of one people, with crimes which he urges them to commit against the lives of others.

But the Southern delegates to the Continental Congress voted against this statement, and it was not included in the final draft of the Declaration. The charges were perhaps true enough, but they did not tell the whole truth. Not mentioned was the fact that Southern slaveowners and slave traders had eagerly cooperated with Britishers engaged in the slavery traffic. And to complicate matters, much of this same slavery traffic was part of the triangular trade that was proving so profitable to the New England merchants.

The charge that King George was "exciting these very people to rise in arms among us" was not completely accurate. About eight months before the Declaration was published, General George Washington had issued an order that his army recruiters were to enlist no young boys, no old men—and no blacks. At the same time Lord Dunmore, British governor of Virginia, declared "all indentured servants, Negroes, or others (appertaining to rebels) free, that are able and willing to bear arms, they joining his Majesty's troops, as soon as may be, for the more speedily reducing this Colony to a proper dignity."

Seeing freedom as their reward, thousands of blacks escaped to fight under the British banner. In time many of the colonial armed forces were thus forced to accept free blacks at first, and later slaves. In all, about

five thousand Negroes served on the American side in the Revolution. They fought with valor in virtually every engagement from Lexington and Concord in 1775 to Yorktown in 1781.

At the end of the war all the slaves among these five thousand were given their freedom as an expression of the nation's gratitude for their service. It was a cue for each Northern state to consider voting for the prohibition of slavery within its borders. In 1780, even before the war was over, Pennsylvania began gradually to abolish slavery. Massachusetts abolished it outright in 1780. Connecticut and Rhode Island introduced gradual abolition in 1784, New York in 1785, New Jersey in 1786. In 1787 Congress included in the Northwest Ordinance a ban on slavery in the whole Northwest Territory, that vast uncharted land north of the Ohio River and east of the Mississippi.

Even the Southern states looked as though they might be easing up on slavery. A number either banned the importation of new blacks from Africa or raised the duty on them to discourage the trade. But the test came at the Constitutional Convention held in Philadelphia during the summer of 1787. Here delegates from twelve states (only Rhode Island absented itself) met to write a new charter for the young United States.

Midway in the seesaw sessions the question arose as to how the slaves were to be considered—as people or as property? The question was a practical one, for the members of the House of Representatives were to be elected on the basis of population: one representative for so many people. The North wanted slaves considered as property, thus cutting down the number of congressmen elected from the South. The South wanted its slaves counted. This would increase the number of congressional districts in the South, each district electing its own representative.

The result was an arithmetical, a fractional, compromise. For the purpose of apportioning representatives, a slave would count as three fifths of a person— five slaves would carry the same weight as three white persons. This was not to say, of course, that a slave could vote. No, indeed. But three fifths of him counted when it came to laying out a congressional district. Was it a small victory for the blacks, a first step on the road to freedom—or was it only a delusion?

And were Southerners seeing an eventual end to slavery when they accepted Article I, Section 9, of the Constitution? This was the provision that prohibited

Congress from banning the importation of slaves until 1808, twenty-one years after the Constitution was written. Did it indicate a light of freedom visible at the end of the tunnel?

But 1808 was years in the future; the tunnel was still long and dark. And Southerners were reassured by the inclusion of this constitutional provision, part of Section 2, Article IV:

"No person held to service or labour in one state, under the laws thereof, escaping into another, shall, in consequence of any law or regulation therein, be discharged from such service or labour, but shall be delivered up on claim of the party to whom such service or labour may be due."

The language is constitutionally polite (notice that the word *slavery* is nowhere used—the substitute is "service or labour"), but the meaning is perfectly clear. A slave who escapes to another state, either slave or free, must be returned to his owner. This was the constitutional basis for the cruel Fugitive Slave Laws of 1793 and 1850. The provision remained in the Constitution until it was blotted out by the Thirteenth Amendment—the history-making amendment passed in 1865 that abolished slavery throughout the United States.

F O U R ☆

Black Uprisings

HOPELESS, HELPLESS, downtrodden, the black slave might have become like a whipped dog. Beaten into submission by the overseer's lash, he might have become dulled, sodden with defeat. But many, if not most, enslaved Negroes maintained their spirit, their humor, and their interest in life. What was more, they fought back in one way or another wherever they could.

Some ran away. At first few runaway slaves got very far. The masters, the sheriffs and deputies, and often the slave hunters with their bloodhounds were soon in hot pursuit. Alone, and unfamiliar with the country-side away from the plantation, the slave was quickly caught. Later, however, many blacks escaped to the northern United States, to Canada, and to Mexico. The local post offices and crossroads general stores in the South were peppered with posters describing fugitive slaves and offering rewards for their capture.

Other slaves, ready to die for freedom, attempted revolts on their own home ground. One historian maintains that there were about 250 slave uprisings before the Civil War. At least three of these rebellions —the ones that took place in 1800, 1822, and 1831 —were etched into public memory for years. All were put down. But each one, in its own twisting and indirect way, helped to bring an end to slavery. All helped to build the road to Sumter.

The first of these uprisings, in 1800, was led by Gabriel Prosser. A long-haired black giant, only twenty-four years old at the time, Prosser was moved and shaken by Bible stories of men who had overthrown their oppressors and triumphed. Inspired by these heroic examples, Prosser plotted to set up a black government in his own state of Virginia. With his brothers, Solomon and Martin, and his wife, Nancy, he prepared to lead black battalions into scenes of Old Testament glory.

Prosser chose Richmond, Virginia's capital, as the

first city to storm and seize. Surveying the city, he studied its accesses and vantage points as well as the location of its arsenals. Then he met secretly with other slaves and planned the attack. Three groups would swoop down on Richmond. One group would commandeer all the firearms in the arsenals. Another group would smash their way into the powder storages. The third was to slay every white person in the city. Only Quakers, Methodists, and Frenchmen were to be spared; these people had performed acts of kindness for the blacks. Later the insurrectionists were to take over other Virginia cities in the same way.

If all went according to plan, Prosser was to be crowned king of Virginia. If the attack went badly, the black armies were to take to the hills and defend themselves to the last.

Everything was ready by the late summer of 1800. A host of slaves—perhaps as few as two thousand or as many as fifty thousand—awaited the signal. The stroke of midnight on August 30 was set as the instant when the revolt was to break into the open.

But the rebellion never even had a chance to begin. It was blocked because two slaves told the story of impending uprising to their masters. The masters, in turn, notified the state authorities. The governor immediately mustered the militia and prepared to put down the revolt.

Prosser did not know he had been informed on. He had gathered a spearhead of a thousand blacks outside Richmond, ready to march on the city. Even though the state's forces had been alerted, the attack might have succeeded. But the white people of Richmond were favored with a second stroke of luck. It rained—in torrents and floods. Roads were washed out, bridges washed away. Prosser had to delay his attack, and before he could regather his forces, he was captured. With thirty odd of his men, he was speedily tried, found guilty, and hanged.

Gabriel Prosser's plan of revolt was rudimentary, and too much depended on chance. This was not true of the well-laid scheme of Denmark Vesey, a free Negro of Charleston, South Carolina.

A big, shrewd man in his early fifties, Vesey had won a lottery twenty-two years before and had been able to buy his freedom. He earned a good living as a carpenter and bought land and buildings. And he hated slavery and slaveowners with a deep and bitter passion. He himself had been owned by a slave trader, and he had seen time and again the miserable agony of the slave auctioned away from his family.

So for years Vesey taught the meaning of freedom and the need for revolt to every slave he could reach. To the blacks he was a magnetic, inspiring figure. Some were more afraid of him than of their masters. He made careful, long-range plans, and by Christmas of 1821 he was ready to move. The plans included a well-organized army with capable leaders commanding the various units. Among his aides were Gullah Jack, who practiced the magic he had learned in Africa; Blind Philip, who could "see" what sighted men could not; and Peter Poyas, a genius at organization.

It was Poyas who worked out the division into units. Only the unit commander was to know the detailed workings of the plan. The blacks under him were to be told only the general purpose of the uprising. Thus if any of them were caught, they could not be forced to confess vital secrets. Most of all, Poyas forbade the recruitment of house servants. These blacks, on friendly terms with their masters, would be more liable to give the plan away.

The recruitment of slaves into Vesey's "army" lasted well into 1822. An estimated nine thousand blacks were enrolled for service in the planned uprising. The target date was set for July 16, a Sunday. On that day Vesey's forces were to capture all the stores of arms and armaments in Charleston, then wipe out the white people. All the whites must be killed, Vesey argued, to insure the safety of the blacks.

But one thing went wrong. A field hand already enrolled tried to enlist a black house servant in the revolt —just what Peter Poyas had warned against. The house servant hurried to his master and recounted all he had learned of the plot. It wasn't much, but it was enough. Thus alerted, the Charleston officials began to investigate.

Each side began stalking the other, waiting like cats to pounce at the critical moment. They circled warily, taking each other's measure. At one stage Poyas and another black leader, Mingo Harth, knew they were under suspicion. Rather than cut and run, they chose to march right down to the mayor's office and demand that they be cleared at once of such unfounded accusations. The city officials, taken aback, let them go free. How could such forthright men possibly be involved in a revolt?

But the end came soon afterward. A slave who knew the details of Vesey's plans, the identity and whereabouts of the leaders, and the locations of the targets, betrayed the plot. Vesey, Poyas, Harth, and most of the other key figures were arrested. Their trials and hangings were swift. All except one of them died without confessing, carrying their cherished secrets into the grave.

The rebellions of Gabriel Prosser and Denmark Vesey were stopped before they got fairly started. The revolt of Nat Turner ran a tragic, murderous course before it was brought to a halt. This uprising struck fear and panic in the hearts of white people throughout the South. Turner's gang killed some sixty white people— and at least a hundred blacks were slain by the hastily mustered white forces that put down the revolt. Another twenty-eight Negroes were convicted of taking part in the uprising. Of these, Turner and twelve others were executed. The rest were deported to Africa.

There was no question of Turner's guilt, nor did he deny his leadership and involvement. Instead, from his cell in the jail at Southampton, Virginia, he dictated a complete confession to his court-appointed white attorney, Thomas R. Gray. The confession, which begins with an account of Turner's life, throws much light on his motives and actions. He tells why he thought his revolt divinely inspired and he himself the instrument of God's will.

At the start of his statement Turner recounts a childhood incident which first convinced him that he had been marked by providence. At the age of three or four he told his playmates of happenings which, his mother vowed, had taken place before he was born. He was sure even then that he "was intended for some great purpose. . . ."

Young Nat learned to read by himself and was busy "making experiments in casting different things in molds made of earth, in attempting to make paper, gunpowder, and many other experiments that, although I could not perfect, yet convinced me of their practicality if I had the means." He was always a dreamer, always taking the hope and the promise for the reality. Yet he was steadily growing in "confidence in my superior judgment" and in the God-sanctioned role he thought he was destined to play.

As a young man he had a vision of what that role was to be: "I saw white spirits and black spirits engaged in battle, and the sun was darkened, the thunder rolled in the heavens, and blood flowed in streams, and I heard a voice saying, 'Such is your luck, such you are called to see, and let it come rough or smooth, you must surely bear it.'"

Turner saw more visions. He became increasingly convinced that he was to lead a great, bloody crusade, ordained and sanctioned by God, to free his fellow slaves: ". . . the Spirit instantly appeared to me and said . . . Christ had laid down the yoke He had borne for the sins of men, and that I should take it on and fight. . . ."

At this point in dictating the confession, Turner was asked by his attorney if he now thought he had been wrong in his beliefs. Turner answered, "Was not Christ crucified?"

An eclipse of the sun in February 1831 was a sign to Turner that the time had come to strike. He revealed his mission to four fellow slaves, Henry, Hark, Nelson, and Sam. They made and rejected several plans. The months dragged on. On August 21 they were joined by two other slaves from the same plantation, Will and Jack. These two demanded action. So the seven determined to begin that same night—by slaying the family of Turner's master, Joseph Travis.

But Nat Turner faltered at the bloody business of killing, and Will had to take over the role as prime executioner. They slew the whole Travis family, and gathering more recruits, proceeded from plantation to plantation on their murderous mission. They were at it all night long, stopping just before dawn to sleep. Soon, however, their sentinels gave the alarm that the white people of the countryside were about to attack.

Nat Turner

Turner and his crew scattered. In time all were captured or slain. Turner hid in the woods for several weeks, living on nuts and berries, but was finally taken. He concluded his confession with the words: "I am here loaded with chains, and willing to suffer the fate that awaits me."

Gray, Turner's attorney, had no reason to believe anything good of his client. Yet even he was forced to admit that Turner "was never known to have a dollar in his life, to swear an oath, or to drink a drop of spirits . . . and for natural intelligence and quickness of apprehension is surpassed by few men I have ever seen. He is a complete fanatic, or plays his part most admirably."

The sentence of death was just. In passing sentence, Jeremiah Cobb, chairman of the court, said that Turner was to blame both for the deaths of the slain whites and for the executions of the blacks under his leadership:

. . . they were your bosom associates; and the blood of all cries aloud, and calls upon you, as the author of their misfortune. Yes! You forced them unprepared, from Time to Eternity. Borne down by this load of guilt, your only justification is, that you were led away by fanaticism. If this be true, from my soul I pity you. . . . The judgment of this court is . . . on Friday next, between the hours of 10 A.M. and 2 P.M., [you shall] be hung by the neck until you are dead! dead! dead! and may the Lord have mercy on your soul.

Three men—Prosser, Vesey, and Turner—were driven to plan mass murder; and one of them, Nat Turner, actually carried out his scheme. There can never be justification or excuse for murder. But the evils of slavery could impel souls in bondage, "led away by fanaticism," to commit such deeds. And today men can begin to see why black slaves in the American South were driven to murder, even at the certain cost of their own lives.

White Advocates
of Black Freedom

THE BLACKS in the United States, both slave and free, did what they could to protest their condition. But they were under severe handicaps. They had no money, no organization, no national leaders, no base of opera-tion. They could not attend a meeting away from their own plantation. Only a few, such as Nat Turner, could read and write.

In the eighteenth and early nineteenth centuries, however, there had been white people in the South—slaveowners themselves—who sincerely believed that slavery must gradually be eliminated. George Wash-ington, who owned many slaves on his Mount Vernon, Virginia, plantation, said: "I can clearly foresee that nothing but the rooting out of slavery can perpetuate the existence of our union by consolidating it in a common bond of principle." Other Southern leaders made similar declarations.

One solution was to return the blacks to Africa, even those who had been born in America. Many white Southerners gathered behind this scheme. In 1817 they founded the American Colonization Society, with Justice Bushrod Washington, a nephew of George Washington's, as president and Henry Clay of Kentucky and John Randolph of Virginia among its members.

The society's plan was to establish a colony called Liberia on the West African coast and to ship American Negroes "home." The colony's capital city was named Monrovia, in honor of President James Monroe, who was inaugurated in 1817, the year of the society's birth. The black "returnees" to Liberia were to be given land and money, and encouraged to start a new life.

Beginning in 1822, some free Negroes were sent to Liberia. Later a few slaves were given their freedom on condition that they settle in the colony. All told, only about twelve thousand blacks made the voyage. Their descendants make up today's leading citizens of Liberia, which has been an independent African republic since 1847.

That was the year when the American Colonization Society finally decided to abandon its efforts and let Liberia go its own way. Yet for thirty years the Society had thought that the blacks "are not, and cannot be, useful and happy among us." Society members sincerely felt "that there should be a separation; that those who are now free, and those who may become so hereafter, should be provided with the means of attaining to a state of respectability and happiness, which, it is certain, they have never yet reached, and, therefore, can never be likely to reach, in this country."

Why did the colonization plan fail? Partly because it was already costing much more than private or government sources were willing to furnish. And partly because its leaders had opposing aims. Some saw in the plan an eventual end to all slavery. Others believed that it was the only answer to the charge that blacks would never become "civilized"—at least according to American standards.

Still others harbored the fond belief that blacks returning to Africa would carry the message of Christianity to that "heathen" continent. And there were those who wanted to rid the United States of all its free Negroes. Then, they thought, the slaves would have no example of freedom to strive for.

Whatever their motives or beliefs, many Southerners until the 1830's believed that the slaves should gradually be *emancipated*—given their freedom. They were deeply troubled by the moral evil that slavery represented, troubled even though their prosperity and their very way of life depended on a system of slave labor.

But two events in the early 1830's brought a sudden change in the attitude of the South. The pro-emancipation people, as well as those who wavered, lined up solidly on the proslavery side because of these two happenings. One was the revolt of Nat Turner in Virginia. The other was the bitter and uncompromising antislavery campaign launched by William Lloyd Garrison and other abolitionists in New England.

Like all great moral issues, slavery—and opposition to slavery—inspired fanaticism and extremism. To be sure, there was some tepid sentiment on both sides. But there were also violent feelings, radicalism on both the left and the right. For his part, Garrison was a firebreathing abolitionist—one who wanted slavery abolished at once, without deals, compromises, or compensation.

William Lloyd Garrison began his career as a teenage printer's apprentice and reporter for the weekly Newburyport (Massachusetts) *Herald.* At twenty-one he started putting out his own weekly *Free Press*. In its pages his opinions and his plan of attack began to take shape. The newspaper failed, but Garrison's zeal mounted. As editor of the *Journal of the Times*, a Vermont weekly, he lashed out against the whole idea of slavery: "We are resolved to agitate the subject to the utmost; nothing but death shall prevent us from denouncing a crime which has no parallel in human depravity."

Wm. Lloyd Garrison

Garrison's papers never had a circulation of more than a few thousand, but his fame grew steadily. In 1829, when he was twenty-three, he was offered the coeditorship of the *Genius of Universal Emancipation*, published in Baltimore, Maryland. Even though he would work in a state where slavery was legal, he did not hesitate to take the assignment. In the very first issue under his editorship he demanded "immediate and unconditional emancipation" for the slaves. Nor did he want the slaveowners reimbursed for freeing their blacks. In a later issue he wrote, "It would be paying a thief for giving up stolen property, and acknowledging that his crime was *not* a crime."

These accusations and indictments got Garrison into deep trouble. He was tried and found guilty of criminal libel, and was sent to jail when he could not pay the fine. Confined for seven weeks, he was freed after his fine was paid by Arthur Tappan, a New Yorker with money and abolitionist sentiments. But another libel charge was hanging over Garrison's head, so he left Baltimore and went to Boston.

Back in New England he made up his mind to launch an all-out newspaper attack on slavery, no holds barred, nothing left unsaid. His new paper was called the *Liberator*; its motto: "Our Country Is the World—

Our Countrymen Are Mankind." And his first editorial
stated his creed:

I *will be* as harsh as truth, and as uncompromising as justice.
On this subject I do not wish to think, or speak, or write,
with moderation. . . . I am in earnest—I will not equivocate
—I will not excuse—I will not retreat a single inch—AND I
WILL BE HEARD.

Young Garrison *was* heard, despite the limited circulation of the *Liberator*. In fact, it was widely believed
that Garrison's writings had incited Nat Turner to his
dark deeds, although there was never any proof that
Turner had ever seen a copy of the *Liberator* or any of
Garrison's earlier papers. Nevertheless every state in
the South banned distribution of the *Liberator*, and
Georgia offered a reward of five thousand dollars for
Garrison's arrest.

Nor were most Northerners very much friendlier to
Garrison. Even those who were against slavery were
put off by Garrison's wrath, his impatience, his harsh
condemnations. He justified (to his own satisfaction, at
least) his impassioned charges by saying, "an immense
iceberg, larger and more impenetrable than any which
floats in the Arctic Ocean, is to be dissolved, and a

little *extra heat* is not only pardonable, but absolutely necessary."

Even avowed Northern abolitionists fought Garrison at first, calling him "the Massachusetts madman." They organized the American Union Against Slavery, a group which was more against Garrison than against black bondage. Garrison shook them off like a horse twitching off flies.

Garrison did not stop with editing and publishing the *Liberator* week after week. He was an active abolitionist organizer and speaker. In 1833 he helped establish the American Anti-Slavery Society and wrote its Declaration of Sentiments. The declaration is a powerful protest against the enslavement of man, stating:

We . . . maintain that no man has a right to enslave . . . his brother; to hold or acknowledge him, for one moment, as a piece of merchandise; to keep back his hire by fraud; or to brutalize his mind by denying him the means of intellectual, social, and moral improvement. . . .

. . . every American citizen who retains a human being in involuntary bondage as his property is (according to Scripture) a MAN STEALER.

. . . the slaves ought instantly to be set free and brought under the protection of law.

And so on, for charge after charge, until the final statement of purpose:

. . . to wipe out the foulest stain which rests upon our national escutcheon; and to secure to the colored population of the United States all the rights and privileges which belong to them as men and as Americans—come what may to our persons, our interests, or our reputations, whether we live to witness the triumph of LIBERTY, JUSTICE, and HUMANITY, or perish untimely as martyrs in this great, benevolent, and holy cause.

The language was direct, the intention noble—and what was more, Garrison meant every word of it. Five years after its founding the American Anti-Slavery Society had 1350 chapters located in all the states of the North, with a heavy concentration in New England.

The struggle between the abolitionists and the proslavery advocates intensified under Garrison's editorial lash. Whatever moral and biblical justification the South may have found for slavery, its real roots lay elsewhere. One root was embedded in the belief that the blacks were "different," and therefore deserved their bondage. Yet the only difference—a meaningless one—was in the color of their skins. All other apparent differences were mainly the result of their enslavement.

Another root was in the economy. With slaves and the cotton gin, there was great wealth to be made by raising cotton. And many of those in the North who tolerated or favored slavery did so because they had lucrative business dealings with prosperous Southern planters.

But with Garrison and his fellow abolitionists, slavery was a burning moral issue. Garrison could not be reasoned with or bought off. Because of all this, he was greatly hated even in his own city of Boston. In fact, at one point Boston merchants who traded with the South swooped down on the *Liberator* office, hitched a rope around Garrison's neck, and dragged him down the street in the direction of the city hall. They may have intended to lynch him then and there. The mayor—whose sentiments were divided—with the help of the police, finally wrestled Garrison away from his kidnapers and put him in jail for his own safety.

In time Garrison realized that the struggle between the forces for and against slavery could end only in civil war. He could see no other solution. In 1842 he changed the *Liberator*'s masthead statement to read: "A repeal of the Union between Northern liberty and Southern slavery is essential to the abolition of the one and the preservation of the other."

The following year he replaced this statement with a resolution passed by the Massachusetts Anti-Slavery Society: "Resolved, That the compact which now exists between the North and South is 'a covenant with death and an agreement with hell'—involving both parties in atrocious criminality and should be immediately annulled."

Garrison added "No Union with Slaveholders!" to the masthead in 1845. And as a triumphant touch he made the final change eight months after the Civil War began in 1861. The concluding declaration was, "Proclaim Liberty throughout all the land, to all the inhabitants thereof." (This classic line, inscribed on Philadelphia's Liberty Bell, is from the Book of Leviticus in the Old Testament.)

In his crusade Garrison made plenty of enemies, but in the end he achieved his aim, and along the way he made a few close friends. One of his greatest admirers was Wendell Phillips, who also became a noted abolitionist leader.

Phillips was a Boston "Brahmin"—an aristocrat descended from the early New England Puritans. Young, wealthy, intelligent, and with a growing law practice, he had every intention and expectation of living a proper Bostonian existence, untouched by the rub and conflict of common life.

That was before he saw Boston businessmen, men he knew and respected, dragging William Lloyd Garrison down the street. The sight sickened him. It also set him thinking. But he did not become an out-and-out abolitionist himself until he married one. His bride was Ann Terry Greene, member of the Female Anti-Slavery Society, and she also had seen Garrison dragged through the streets. Two years later she and Phillips were married. Phillips always gave his wife full credit for his "conversion": "My wife made an out-and-out abolitionist out of me, and she always preceded me in the adoption of the various causes I have advocated."

Another incident helped Phillips take the plunge into the sea of abolitionist activity. In 1837, the same year that he and Miss Greene were married, Elijah P. Lovejoy was slain. Lovejoy was a crusading abolitionist newspaper editor in Alton, Illinois, above St. Louis on the Illinois side of the Mississippi. Illinois was a free state, but Missouri, just west across the wide river, was a slave state. And a proslavery mob murdered Lovejoy. His death became a rallying cry for the whole abolitionist movement, uniting the warring factions and helping them to forget their differences.

To denounce Lovejoy's murder, an abolitionist group assembled in Boston's Faneuil Hall to listen to several

speakers. One of them, however, turned out to be a proslavery man. He was James T. Austin, attorney general of Massachusetts, and for a time he seemed to be making good sense. That was until Wendell Phillips rushed to the lectern. Unable to stomach Austin's tirade against abolitionism, Phillips demolished with logic and eloquence each charge in turn.

As a result of this impromptu speech, Phillips found that many old friends and powerful clients had suddenly turned against him. He also found that he had become one of the chief leaders of the abolitionist cause. On balance, he felt that he had gained far more than he had lost.

Wendell Phillips never considered that he needed a majority behind him. He said, "The reformer . . . disregards popularity and deals only with ideas, conscience, and common sense." On another occasion he remarked, "I am not to be bullied by institutions. I am not to be frightened by parchments. Forms and theories are nothing to me. Majorities are nothing." What the abolitionists lacked in numbers, they made up for by furious activity.

Still, during much of the 1840's and 1850's, the abolitionists (despite their more than a thousand local chapters) were scattered thinly through the Northern states. They had relatively few sympathizers in Congress and in their state legislatures. Too many people, in government and out, still felt that if the Southern states wanted slavery, it was their right to have it. They believed that each state had the right to decide the question for itself—and that it was no business of the federal government to interfere in the decision.

For the most part, then, the North turned its back on the slavery problem. It was not their concern—or so most people insisted on believing. But this belief was not a deep-dyed conviction—and the time was coming when their minds could and would be changed. The nation was well started along the road to Sumter.

Douglass, Then Lincoln

Two MEN did much in the 1840's and 1850's to rouse the Northern politicians and voters into realizing that it was the federal government's responsibility to do something about slavery. One of them was Frederick Douglass, a black abolitionist who had been born a slave. The other was Abraham Lincoln, a lawyer and legislator who had been born south of Mason and Dixon's Line.

Douglass' father was white. In his autobiography, written in 1845, Douglass said: "Of my father I know nothing. Slavery had no recognition of fathers, as none of families. That the mother was a slave was enough for its deadly purpose. By its law the child followed the condition of its mother. The father might be a freeman and the child a slave. The father might be a white man, glorying in the purity of his Anglo-Saxon blood, and the child ranked with the blackest slaves. Father he might be, and not be husband, and could sell his own child without incurring reproach, if in its veins coursed one drop of African blood."

Young Frederick grew up on a plantation in Talbot County, Maryland. As a child he had only a shirt to wear, summer and winter. On cold nights he covered himself with a sack. He and the other black children were fed cornmeal mush poured into a common trough. Like pigs the children had to fight for their share.

Then when he was eight years old, Frederick became a house servant to a Baltimore family. His mistress, Mrs. Hugh Auld—"Miss Sopha"—taught him to read, until her husband forced her to stop. The boy learned to write by studying the carpenter's marks at Hugh Auld's shipyard. And he learned about freedom from a schoolbook, *The Columbian Orator*, which he bought for fifty cents with money he had earned by shining shoes. The book was full of speeches given by noted Englishmen on the subject of human liberty.

The book set young Douglass to giving his own speeches to his fellow slaves. For this, his master turned

Frederick
Douglass

Douglass over to a "slave-breaker," whose job was to break the spirit of black troublemakers. Twice the boy tried to escape. The second time he succeeded. He made his way to New Bedford, Massachusetts, and found work in a shipyard. His pay was a dollar a day—and it was all his own money.

Douglass' career as an abolitionist started when he was twenty-four. At an antislavery convention held in Nantucket, Massachusetts, he was asked to say a few words about his life as a slave. The nervousness and trembling he felt when he got up to address an audience of white strangers soon gave way to a magnificent eloquence. He became a professional speaker for the antislavery movement, traveling a good deal in the northern United States and in Europe, especially in England. In 1846 his English friends bought him his freedom by paying 150 pounds (about $750) to the Auld family.

Taking his place beside Garrison, Phillips, and many others, Douglass carried the fight for black freedom to every group who would listen. He published his own abolitionist paper, *North Star*, and won more and more support. In time, however, he parted with the white abolitionists, for he wanted more than legal freedom for his people. He demanded that they be treated as equals. It was a demand that much of today's white world is still not ready to grant.

But Douglass' seemingly outrageous demands caused the white world of his time to take a long look at its own responsibilities toward the blacks. Gradually many white people of the North began to realize that the responsibility was a collective one, the duty of the federal government. This realization did not take shape until the late 1850's, and it owed much to Douglass' persuasion.

Frederick Douglass was an impassioned pleader for justice. Abraham Lincoln was a logical debater who based his arguments on the law and the Constitution.

In one sense Lincoln, who was born in Kentucky, might have been considered a Southerner. For Kentucky, a border state south of the Ohio River, was usually Southern in its ideas and attitudes. In another sense, however, Lincoln was always a man of the Middle West. When he was only seven, his family struck out for the Indiana frontier. When he was twenty-one, the Lincolns moved westward again, this time to central Illinois. Young Lincoln settled in the little town of New Salem, on the Sangamon River. For the next thirty years he lived in New Salem or in the nearby growing community of Springfield.

Thus Lincoln grew up and spent his maturing years in the country's great middle region. There, beyond the populous East, away from the slaveholding South, but short of the still lawless West, people were exposed to few political extremes. Lincoln himself was no radical of the left or the right, neither a fiery abolitionist nor a staunch proslavery advocate. Only one idea ruled, one passion was paramount: respect for the law.

This respect for the nation's laws—for the very idea of law itself—was a long time developing in Abe Lincoln. As a boy and young man he had to fight hard to acquire the scraps of book learning available on the frontier. He had been a farmer, storekeeper, river boatman, rail-splitter, and even—during the brief Black Hawk War of 1832—an Indian fighter. That same year he ran for a seat in the Illinois state legislature but lost. Two years later he ran again. This time he won. From the beginning he was a shrewd and able legislator, guiding bills through the chamber with a sure hand.

At the same time he was reading law, preparing himself to be a lawyer. In 1836 the Sangamon Circuit Court certified him as a man of good moral character, the first step toward admission to the Illinois bar. He took the bar examination in the summer of that year, and in September he was admitted to practice.

Lincoln was always a "public man," always involved in community life, always with his finger on the public pulse. The year after he became a lawyer, abolitionist editor Elijah P. Lovejoy was murdered in nearby Alton, and young Lincoln's crusading sense was aroused. Eleven weeks after the slaying, he spoke before the Young Men's Lyceum in Springfield. His theme was not the brutality of the crime as such, but the violation of the rule of law. He saw in the killing an abandonment of the agreement among men to live in peace and under law, a move by the "mobocratic spirit" to wreck the legally appointed government.

Then only twenty-eight, Lincoln was already setting down guidelines for his policies and pronouncements of twenty-five years later. He said, "There is no grievance that is a fit object of redress by mob law. In any case that arises, as for instance, the promulgation of abolitionism, one of two positions is necessarily true: that is, the thing is right within itself, and therefore deserves the protection of all law and good citizens; or it is wrong, and therefore proper to be prohibited by legal enactments; and in neither case is the interposition of mob law either necessary, justifiable, or excusable."

Even then, he was pleading to let law rule, to live by compact and agreement. He closed by saying: "Let every American, every lover of liberty, every well-wisher to his posterity, swear by the blood of the Revolution, never to violate in the least particular, the laws of the country; and never to tolerate their violation by others. Let reverence for the laws . . . become the *political religion* of the nation. . . ."

It was this "political religion" that motivated Lincoln as lawyer, legislator, and finally as President. He was careful and cautious, always working within the law, never seeking solutions outside the great codes laid down to govern the conduct of men in society.

Lincoln served four terms in the Illinois state legislature, but this body actually met for only a few months during each two-year term. His main job was working as a lawyer "on the circuit." The judges moved from town to town along a set route, or circuit, holding court for a few days or weeks in each place. Lincoln and his lawyer friends followed the judges, pleading cases before them in the various communities.

At least two of Lincoln's cases in the 1840's involved blacks. But his pleadings in both cases were neither *for* nor *against* the Negroes, but *for* the law.

One such case was *Bailey* v. *Cromwell*. Cromwell had sold a black girl to Bailey, both assuming at the time that she was a slave. Bailey then gave a promissory note in payment—the cash itself was to come later. But Lincoln argued before the Illinois Supreme Court that the girl, unless it could be proved that she was a slave, was free. As such, she could not be bought or sold. The court agreed that she was to be considered free and "could not be the subject of a sale." Thus the promissory note, the subject of the suit, was ruled to be "illegal."

In the Matson case Lincoln defended the right of a Kentucky slaveowner to bring his slaves into Illinois, even though Illinois law said that all slaves living in the state for a year or more had to be set free. Lincoln's argument did not challenge the law. His only plea was that there was no legal proof that Matson's slaves had been in Illinois for a year. The court, however, decided against Lincoln.

In both cases—one for a black's freedom, the other to keep blacks enslaved—Lincoln was on the side of the law. If a black was entitled to his freedom under Illinois law, then Lincoln was for freedom. But if, under Illinois law, a slave could not prove his right to his own freedom, then Lincoln was for the law.

Lincoln was still young, still growing, and he was yet to appear on the national scene. Yet he was convinced even then that the law must be permitted to fulfill its responsibility. In time he would lead this nation through a civil war fought to preserve the lawfully conceived federal union.

SEVEN

Two Compromises

DURING MUCH of the first half of the nineteenth century, hardheaded Northern businessmen generally got along well with Southern planters. But equally hardheaded Northern congressmen were usually at odds with Southern representatives and senators. The issues in Congress were often based on slavery, but the question of whether slavery was right or wrong was rarely raised.

One of the reasons why North-South political relationships were so contrary was that the South had an extra Constitutional advantage because of its slaves. Each slave was worth three fifths of a person when it came to counting people in order to decide the number of representatives each state was entitled to have in Congress. The same three-fifths ratio applied in choosing electors for the electoral college.

In 1789, when the Constitution was adopted, the populations of the North and South were about equal. But by 1820 the free states had forged ahead. They had a total population, according to the 1820 census, of 5,152,000, while the slave states had 4,485,000, including slaves.

In 1820, the North had 105 seats in the House of Representatives. The South had 81, but this was more than it would have had if slaves had not been counted as part of its population. In the Senate, however, by the admission of one new slave state for each new free state, there was an equal balance among the senators representing the twenty-two states of the Union in 1819. These twenty-two states occupied almost all the land east of the Mississippi, except for the Wisconsin Territory. Part of Louisiana extended west of the Mississippi, the only state at this time beyond the broad river.

Louisiana, carved from the vast Louisiana Territory, had entered the Union as a slave state in 1812. During the next several years slaveowners from the state of Louisiana moved farther north and settled along the lower Missouri River or near the city of St. Louis, located just below where the Missouri joins the Mississippi. Thus when Missouri asked to join the Union, it wanted to be admitted as a slave state.

But Missouri lay north of the line—the extension of the old Mason and Dixon's Line and the Ohio River—that until now had divided the slaveholding from the free states. Did this mean that slavery was about to work its way north? Did this mean that the slave states, though smaller in white population, would gain control of Congress because of their "three-fifths" advantage?

There was hot debate in the state legislatures, in newspapers, and at public meetings. And the arguments were not over whether slavery itself was good or evil, but rather whether the slave states would take command of Congress and control the election of the President.

In the end Congress, in admitting Missouri, tried to please both sides. Missouri was accepted as a slave state. And Maine—which had just split off from Massachusetts—came in as a free state. Thus was the balance kept even, 12 to 12.

But Congress, in the legislation that became known as the Missouri Compromise, also stated that slavery should be banned from that portion of the Louisiana Purchase lying north of the line 36° 30′, Missouri's southern boundary. The South seemed satisfied, for Arkansas and Florida, about ready to enter the Union, would come in as slave states. The North seemed equally satisfied. Most of the unsettled U.S. territories lay north of the compromise line and thus would enter as free states when they were ready. It looked as though this Missouri Compromise of 1820 would hold good for a very long time.

The Missouri Compromise was, however, a *political* deal. It failed to face up to the *moral* issue of slavery. Old Thomas Jefferson, writing a letter from his Monticello plantation in Virginia, was deeply disturbed over what this failure meant: ". . . this momentous question, like a fire bell in the night, awakened and filled me with terror. I considered it at once as the knell of the Union."

John Quincy Adams took an equally dim view of the Missouri Compromise. In the nation's capital—he was then Secretary of State under President James Monroe and would be President himself after him—he wrote in his diary: "I have favored this Missouri Compromise, believing it to be all that could be effected under the present Constitution, and from ex-

treme unwillingness to put the Union at hazard. . . .
[But] if the Union is to be dissolved, slavery is pre-
cisely the question on which it ought to break. For the
present, however, this contest is laid asleep."

Did the road to Fort Sumter start at the Missouri
Compromise?

The first challenge to the Union after the Missouri
Compromise did not arise, however, from the slavery
issue. It came from the state of South Carolina over a
controversy on *tariffs*—taxes on imported goods. Under President John Quincy Adams, Congress passed a
"protective" tariff law with the idea of discouraging
the importation of manufactured goods from England.
Its purpose was to protect American manufacturers
from English competition. But England was one of
South Carolina's best customers for raw cotton. If England couldn't sell its manufactured goods in the United
States, it couldn't afford to buy cotton from South
Carolina.

It was now 1828, and Andrew Jackson was running
against Adams for the Presidency. Jackson's backers in
Congress figured on a sure-fire way to earn votes for
their man. They would offer a new tariff bill in Congress, one that would tax imported raw materials as
well as manufactured goods. They expected the bill to

be so outrageous that if it passed, Adams would surely veto it—and thus be in trouble with the American producers of raw materials. This "tariff of abominations" did pass. Adams, contrary to expectations, signed it. And he was in trouble, especially in the South.

South Carolina vowed it was all a plot on the part of New England manufacturers to rob the state of its English customers. South Carolinians blamed all their troubles on the bill. Many actually talked about quitting the Union. There were similar, but more muted, rumblings from men in other Southern states.

One South Carolina leader was John C. Calhoun, Vice-President under Adams. Calhoun wanted to run for Vice-President on Jackson's ticket. He needed Jackson's support, and he needed the support as well of those South Carolinians who wanted to take their state out of—secede from—the Union. But their proposed method of secession was revolutionary. It meant taking the law into their own hands. So Calhoun hunted for a legal alternative to the idea of secession.

Calhoun spent the summer of 1828 on his South Carolina plantation, thinking and jotting down his thoughts. There he thought he had found a lawful and constitutional alternative in his theory of *nullification*. For this theory he worked out several arguments:

1. The Constitution of the United States, Calhoun asserted, was originally a compact between the thirteen sovereign states and the federal government, whereby each state retained forever its "sovereignty"—its individual identity and rights. Therefore the people of a state have the right to *nullify*—cancel—a law passed by Congress if they are convinced the federal government has exceeded its authority.

2. Such a protective tariff is both unconstitutional and unfair to South Carolina. It protects Northern manufacturers but not South Carolina cotton planters, who must sell their crop abroad. South Carolina thus has the right, if it chooses to use it, of nullifying the tariff law.

3. For the present, however, South Carolina should take no action, giving Congress itself a chance to amend the law. The threat of nullification would be enough at this time.

Calhoun had his reasons for being so cautious. He had hopes that Jackson as President would act to reduce the effects of the "tariff of abominations." Calhoun would then earn the reputation of being Jackson's trusted aide and adviser. Seeing one of their own in such a key position, South Carolina and the other cotton-growing states would calm down. And when Jackson was ready to step down from the Presidency, by the end of his second term at the latest, Calhoun would step up.

But Calhoun's well-laid plans did not work out. He and Jackson became entangled in a number of quarrels over which came first, the state or the nation. Jackson, although he believed in states' rights, was all for federal supremacy. Calhoun, however, took the opposite view. He said: "I never use the word 'nation' in speaking of the United States. I always use the word 'union' or 'confederacy.' We are not a nation, but a *union*, a confederacy of equal and sovereign states."

As Vice-President, Calhoun was also the presiding officer of the Senate. Right on the Senate floor he met strong opposition to his views. For example, on one occasion he heard Senator Robert Y. Hayne of South Carolina make a speech about nullification. When Hayne had finished, Daniel Webster, the senator from Massachusetts and a great orator in the old style, rose to answer. Webster spoke for hours without pausing, mixing in poetry, humor, facts, and criticism of what he called the "South Carolina" doctrine. He closed with a tumbling cascade of rhetoric:

When my eyes shall be turned to behold for the last time the sun in heaven, may I not see him shining on the broken and dishonored fragments of a once glorious Union; on States dissevered, discordant, belligerent; on a land rent with civil feuds, or drenched, it may be, in fraternal blood! Let their last feeble and lingering glance rather behold the gorgeous ensign of the republic, now known and honored throughout the earth, still full high advanced, its arms and trophies streaming in their original lustre, not a stripe erased or polluted, nor a single star obscured, bearing for its motto, no such miserable interrogatory as 'What is all this worth?' nor those other words of delusion and folly, 'Liberty first and Union afterwards'; but everywhere, spread all over in characters of living light, blazing on all its ample folds, as they float over the sea and over the land, and in every wind under the whole heavens, that other sentiment, dear to every true American heart,—Liberty *and* Union, now and forever, one and inseparable!

Webster's rich prose did not discourage Calhoun. President Jackson's comment on the doctrine of nullification was more terse. At a Jefferson Day banquet a little while after Webster's speech, Jackson looked directly at Calhoun as he offered the toast: "Our Federal Union! It *must* and *shall be* preserved!"

In 1832, Congress did something about revising the tariff of abominations—but not enough to satisfy most

South Carolinians. Now was the time, they thought, to put nullification to work. They voted to nullify both the original tariff of abominations and its revisions. To give their state a proper voice in Congress, they elected Calhoun to the Senate. Calhoun resigned as Vice-President—the only Vice-President ever to do so—in order to take his seat as senator.

President Jackson was in no mood for such foolishness. He asked Congress to pass a force bill, authorizing him to use the army and navy to enforce the nation's laws in South Carolina. Congress passed the bill—and at the same time it put through a compromise tariff bill. South Carolina, liking the compromise, repealed its own nullification act. In doing so, it nullified Jackson's force bill, which could only go into action if South Carolina actually defied federal law. (During the crisis hour before Fort Sumter fell, President Lincoln asked Congress to pass a similar force bill, permitting him to use the army to enforce federal law in South Carolina. Congress refused.)

So South Carolina's nullification notions petered out. Calhoun looked for another political issue that would keep him in the forefront of public attention. He found it in slavery. Jackson had freely predicted that

Calhoun would do so. The next excuse for Calhoun's antifederal government activities, said Jackson, would be "the Negro, or slavery question."

Slavery soon became a burning issue in Congress, because the abolitionists decided to focus their attack on the District of Columbia—an area which Congress, under the Constitution, controlled. Washington had become an auction center and shipping point for newly purchased slaves destined for the Deep South. From the windows of the Capitol, congressmen could see armed guards escorting bands of shackled slaves. The silence of the congressmen was a license for slave traders to continue their dealings in Washington.

The abolitionists, eager to wipe out slavery in the District, deluged Congress with petitions. Many Southerners were equally determined to see slavery continue in the national capital. It became a point of honor with them. Calhoun said that any interference with slavery in the District of Columbia was a "foul slander on nearly one-half the States of the Union."

Most congressmen paid little or no attention to the antislavery petitions. But the South was worried about their possible effect. So a group of determined Southern congressmen rammed a "gag resolution" through the House of Representatives. The rule said that all antislavery petitions had to be "tabled"—that is, put away without being considered.

Some Northern congressmen hated the gag rule. They thought it encroached on their rights and obligations as lawmakers. Leading the fight against the resolution was John Quincy Adams, now in his seventies. After he left the Presidency in 1829, Adams had been elected to the House of Representatives. There he became known as "Old Man Eloquent," not because his voice was melodious (it was actually cracked and harsh), but because of his bristling attacks on what he considered to be evils in government. To him the gag rule was a prime evil, and he fought it with all his strength. He would not be silenced, and he knew every trick in the parliamentary rules' book that would enable him to take the floor. It took several years, but he finally brought the House around to his way of thinking. In 1844 the gag rule was repealed.

It was by such back-door routes as repeal of the gag rule that Congress approached its responsibility towards slavery. Yet slavery and slave trading were not abolished in the District of Columbia at this time. For the present, Calhoun and his cohorts had won. But their time of victory was running out.

The Mexican War started in 1846. The United States went to war with its neighbor to the south for a variety of reasons, most of them suspect. There were questions of disputed boundaries and territories, and alleged debts owed Americans by Mexicans.

American leaders, looking ahead, knew that the United States would surely conquer. They saw that California and much of the Southwest, then owned by Mexico, would be handed over to the victor. These would become part of the United States as territories and, in time, states.

It was at this stage that Congressman David Wilmot of Pennsylvania offered a resolution, as part of another bill then before the House, that slavery should be banned in any new territory, North or South, acquired by federal funds. This "Wilmot Proviso" meant that Southerners could not take their slaves into the newly acquired lands; it also meant that when the new territories entered the Union as free states, the balance between free and slave states in the Senate would be upset.

For this reason Calhoun fought savagely against Wilmot's resolution and for "equality"—the balance of senators. He argued: "I am a Southern man and a slaveholder—a kind and merciful one, I trust—and none the worse for being a slaveholder. I say, for one,

I would rather meet any extremity upon earth than give up one inch of our equality—one inch of what belongs to us as members of this great republic!" The measure passed the House, but it was defeated in the Senate.

The Mexican War ended in 1848, and, as predicted, California and the Southwest were the spoils of war. Then the news was out that gold had been discovered in California, and the rush was on. Thousands of gold seekers flocked to the territory, and many were ready to settle there permanently. By 1850 California was asking to be admitted to the Union as a state.

Before California could be admitted, however, a number of questions had to be worked out—mainly slavery-based questions. Both North and South had to be satisfied, at least in part, with the solution. It took Henry Clay of Kentucky, Daniel Webster, and Stephen A. Douglas, a new senator from Illinois, to work out the now historic Compromise of 1850.

To please the South, the state of Texas (which had entered the Union only five years before) was awarded ten million dollars to compensate for giving up all claims to the new New Mexico Territory. A stricter Fugitive Slave Law was passed, imposing heavy penalties on persons who helped a slave escape or who interfered with his capture.

For the North, slave trading (but not slavery itself) was banned in the District of Columbia. California was admitted as a free state. And the question of slavery was not mentioned in the organization of the New Mexico and Utah territories.

Calhoun, of course, was not satisfied with what the South was offered. But Calhoun was dying. Too weak to speak from the floor himself, he had another senator, James M. Mason, read his speech for him. Yet his demands, as always, were strong. In order to preserve the

J. C. Calhoun

Union, he had written, the abolitionist movement must be declared illegal. Southerners should have equal rights in the territories, which meant they should be allowed to take their slave property anywhere. And the Constitution must be amended to offer safeguards to the South.

He did not reveal in the speech what that amendment should actually be. It was the most extreme idea of all. The United States should elect two Presidents, one from the North, one from the South. Each President was to have full power to veto any new law passed by Congress.

Calhoun wanted the South to stay in the Union, but only on its own terms. If those terms were not met, the South would leave the Union, he said. And if the North attempted to block this secession, the only answer was civil war.

Less than a month after Calhoun's speech was delivered, he was dead. But the chance for a permanent peaceful solution to the growing rift between the North and the South had died long before. The Compromise of 1850 only postponed the Civil War for another decade.

Abraham Lincoln had been against the Mexican War. He had served one term in Congress (1847–49) as representative from the Illinois Seventh Congressional District. When he came to Washington, the war was just about over. Lincoln kept charging that the United States was waging an illegal war and should withdraw without claiming as its own any new territory. His stand was extremely unpopular with the voters from his congressional district, which had furnished many troops for the Mexican campaign. He failed to win reelection.

Lincoln welcomed the Compromise of 1850, as did most of the people in the United States—except, of course, the rampant abolitionists. He hoped that the compromise's complex of laws and agreements would perhaps permanently "contain" slavery in an expanding United States. When Henry Clay died in 1852, Lincoln praised him: ". . . he did not perceive, as I think no wise man has perceived, how it [slavery] could be *at once* eradicated, without producing a greater evil, even to the cause of human liberty."

Abraham Lincoln had not yet arrived at his final position on slavery and the Union. But he was drawing close.

EIGHT ☆

Kansas and Nebraska

IN 1852 the voters of the United States elected Franklin Pierce, a Democrat from New Hampshire, as President. He won a landslide victory largely because he was "safe." He had made no strong pro- or anti-slavery campaign statements, and most voters in both the North and the South had a feeling that the slavery question had died down. After all, hadn't the Compromise of 1850 settled matters to every thinking man's satisfaction?

The slavery question, in reality, remained unsolved. This seemed to bother only the abolitionists, who kept pointing out that slavery was morally wrong. But the dedicated abolitionists were relatively few in number.

Most antislavery Northerners were chiefly concerned with the possibility that the slave states would grow more numerous and thus take over the Congress and the Presidency. In particular, they did not want slavery to expand into the new territories that had been marked off as free by the Missouri Compromise of 1820.

But new history is always being made. President Pierce's Secretary of War, Jefferson Davis (a Mississippian who later was to be president of the Confederacy), had a surprise announcement to make. The government planned to build the first transcontinental railroad. It was to start in Memphis, Tennessee, and follow a southerly route to the Pacific coast. The meaning of this plan was obvious. It would link the Southern slave states with the new Southwest territories —and when the latter made their bid for entry into the Union as states, they would tend to come in as slave.

Davis even persuaded President Pierce to buy a piece of Mexican-owned land in southern Arizona in order to lay out the best southern right-of-way. This Gadsden Purchase (named for James Gadsden, who negotiated the deal) cost the United States ten million dollars.

But before plans for a Southern transcontinental

line could progress much further, Senator Stephen A. Douglas of Illinois stepped into the proceedings. The "Little Giant" (he was five feet four inches tall) represented those Northerners who felt that the South, by its railroad plans, was ready to push slavery beyond the "containment" limits.

Douglas also represented Chicago railroad and real estate interests with ideas of their own. They wanted a transcontinental railroad that would start in Chicago and pass through the Nebraska and Wyoming regions on its way west to California. Of the two groups Douglas represented, the Chicago investors were much the stronger.

The Little Giant was representing still another interest—his own. He was aiming for the Presidency in 1856.

Douglas was chairman of the Senate Committee on Territories. He knew that if the railroad was to follow a mid-continental route, the areas it passed through would first have to be organized as federal territory. And whether slavery was to be permitted there would have to be settled one way or another.

So in 1854 Douglas offered a bill in the Senate for the organization of the Great Plains region into the territory of Nebraska. Other bills to accomplish this had been offered before. But Southern senators had voted them down because the bills prohibited slavery. This ban was in line with the Missouri Compromise of 1820, which had prohibited slavery north of the westward extension of Missouri's southern boundary, except for Missouri itself. To please both Southern and Northern backers, Douglas consented to dividing the proposed territory in two—the northern half as Nebraska, the southern half as Kansas.

To make sure his bill passed, Douglas changed the rules. The new bill provided that the people of the Kansas and Nebraska territories were to decide for themselves whether or not they wanted slavery. Douglas defended this new feature by calling it popular sovereignty; it was soon nicknamed "squatter sovereignty."

But popular or squatter sovereignty was not enough for the Southern congressmen, even though it had the effect of cutting the muscle out of the Missouri Compromise. They wanted more. They wanted the Missouri Compromise written out of the statute books. They wanted it *repealed*—canceled. So Douglas agreed to the repeal of the Missouri Compromise. With this, the Kansas-Nebraska Act of 1854 was passed.

The new law, however, was too much for some

Northern leaders. Senator Salmon P. Chase of Ohio wrote a strong protest that was signed by other anti-slavery senators and congressmen, and widely printed and reprinted. Chase denounced the Kansas-Nebraska Act as a threat to freedom and to the Union itself. The new law, he said, would turn the West into "a dreary region of despotism, inhabited by masters and slaves." He also warned that the law was a plot to keep out free workers from the Northeast, as well as settlers from Europe. Chase's protest echoed a feeling rapidly spreading in the North that the South was trying to take over the federal government.

The Kansas-Nebraska Bill of 1854 aroused Abraham Lincoln as no other political issue had ever done before. Three months after the bill became law, Lincoln was back in politics.

Before 1854 American voters were united in loose groups with shifting political allegiances. They would rally behind one party banner, then another, depending on the issues and the personality of the candidate. But the passage of the Kansas-Nebraska Act forced a true realignment of parties.

In many states the antislavery Whigs, Free-Soilers (those who backed a free Kansas and Nebraska), abolitionists, and Northern Democrats gathered to form a new party, the Republican. The main strength of the Democratic party was now largely in the South. (Another new party also emerged at this time: the American, or Know-Nothing, party. This was a bigoted, ignorant group that catered to prejudice and intolerance. It got its nickname from the fact that its members when questioned about the party's aims or organization were instructed to say, "I know nothing.")

Lincoln was a Whig, and he hung onto the party affiliation after the party itself had ceased to function effectively. In time, however, he became a Republican. His return to politics in 1854 was not at first to make a bid for office himself. Instead he stumped for the re-election of Congressman Richard Yates of Jacksonville, Illinois, who had fought against the passage of the Kansas-Nebraska Act. For Yates's valiant action against his fellow Illinoisian, Stephen Douglas, Lincoln felt that he deserved to be returned to Congress.

As a political person himself, Lincoln had grown tremendously since his days in the Illinois legislature and in Congress. The whole idea of the Kansas-Nebraska Act and its popular sovereignty—letting the people of a new territory decide for themselves whether to be slave or free—repelled him. His logical, legalistic mind reasoned that in order to preserve the Union slavery would have to be permitted in all the states— or banned in all of them. Yet was the nation ready for such a momentous choice?

Stephen Douglas came to Springfield to defend his Kansas-Nebraska Act, and Lincoln was called on to answer him. It was October 3, 1854, and the town was crowded with visitors to the annual Illinois State Fair. In his speech before the fair-going crowd, Douglas asserted that the Missouri Compromise of 1820 had been unfair. Furthermore, he said, the Compromise of 1850 had actually introduced the idea of popular sovereignty. The Kansas-Nebraska Act was only applying the idea to a new region. Besides, he claimed, neither Kansas nor Nebraska would ever adopt slavery. The soil and the weather, he reassured his audience, were all wrong for slave-labor crops.

The next evening Lincoln delivered his public reply to Douglas, who sat listening attentively in the front row of the chamber of the state legislature. Without coat, collar, or cravat—it was a hot night, and the hall was packed—Lincoln began slowly and soberly. He opened by branding slavery itself as a "monstrous injustice," but denied any prejudice towards the Southern people for keeping slaves. And he confessed his own

inability to solve the slavery problem. Shipping the slaves to the American Colonization Society's Liberia had not been the answer. Nor was it in freeing them all immediately and treating them as equals.

Yet a black was a human being, deserving at least gradual emancipation and a certain voice in governing himself. "The doctrine of self-government is right, absolutely and eternally right—but it has no just application as here attempted," he said.

"Or perhaps . . . ," Lincoln went on, "whether it has such just application depends on whether a Negro is *not* or *is* a man. If he is *not*, why in that case he who *is* a man may, as a matter of self-government, do just as he pleases with him. But if the Negro *is* a man, is it not . . . a total destruction of self-government, to say that he too shall not govern himself? . . . If the Negro is a *man*, why then my ancient faith teaches me that 'all men are created equal,' and that there can be no moral right in connection with one man's making a slave of another."

What then was the answer? Lincoln was not ready to push for the ultimate choice—a nation all slave or all free. At this time he wanted only to restore the Missouri Compromise, "contain" slavery, let it expand no farther. "Let us turn slavery from its claims of 'moral right' back upon its existing legal rights and its arguments of 'necessity.' Let us return it to the position our fathers gave it, and there let it rest in peace. . . ."

In short, Lincoln knew full well that slavery was a great evil. But to him, breaking up the Union was an even greater evil. At this time he was willing to accept one great evil for the sake of blocking an even greater evil.

In 1855, the year after his reply to Douglas, Lincoln was a candidate for the United States Senate. Until the Seventeenth Amendment to the Constitution was adopted in 1913, senators were chosen by their state legislatures. In a close legislative election Lincoln was defeated. But he did not give up political activity; he was too involved in the great issues of his time. For the moment he had no personal ambition for political office. But he meant to go on speaking about the grave problems that assailed his country. Whether he knew it or not, Lincoln was already on the road to Sumter.

Polarization Proceeds

AMONG ITS other flaws, the Kansas-Nebraska Act
triggered deep resentment over the Fugitive Slave Law,
which had been one of the features of the Compromise
of 1850. When that compromise bill was passed, most
Northerners had been willing to accept its provisions
in the interests of keeping the peace. But the resentment aroused by the Kansas-Nebraska Act caused people to look again at the slave-catching law and to see
its many evils. Among them: an accused fugitive had
no right to a trial by jury; he could not summon wit-
nesses to testify in defense of himself; and if captured,
he could again be enslaved, even though he had es-

caped long before the Fugitive Slave Law went into effect.

Ralph Waldo Emerson, renowned New England writer and speaker, had not aligned himself with the abolitionists until now. Shaken by the exposure of the oppressive features of the Fugitive Slave Law, he said:

. . . The way in which the country was dragged to consent to this, and the disastrous defection (on the miserable cry of Union) of the men of letters, of the colleges, of educated men, nay, of some preachers of religion, was the darkest passage in the history. It showed that our prosperity hurt us, and that we could not be shocked by crime. It showed that the old religion and the sense of the right had faded and gone out; that while we reckoned ourselves a highly cultivated nation, our bellies had run away with our brains, and the principles of culture and progress did not exist.

The day after the Kansas-Nebraska Act was passed, a belligerent band in Boston tried to free Anthony Burns, a black fugitive about to be returned South to his master. It took a battalion of United States soldiers and four platoons of marines to "protect" the slave as he was marched to a ship at the wharf. Twenty-two companies of Massachusetts state militia were called out to hold back the angry, booing crowds that lined the streets. John Greenleaf Whittier, the good gray New England poet, wrote of the scene:

And, as I thought of Liberty
Marched handcuffed down that sworded street
The solid earth beneath my feet
Reeled fluid as the sea.

It was the last time in Massachusetts that a runaway slave was handed over to his master. The North was beginning to be thoroughly aroused over the slavery issue. It was beginning to see that slavery was not only a political danger—it was also a moral wrong.

Then there were the Northern merchants who had once been in sympathy with the Southern planters. They too opposed the Kansas-Nebraska Act because it threatened to upset the balance between free and slave states. They had tolerated slavery as long as only a minority of citizens held the right to own or trade slaves and only a balanced number of states could send slavery senators to Washington. Now, with that balance in jeopardy, they began to consider the evils of slavery itself.

And a book published two years earlier had already gripped millions of readers who had never before thought of what being a slave really meant. The book

was *Uncle Tom's Cabin,* and the author was Harriet Beecher Stowe. More thousands were seeing the story acted out on the stage as a play.

Uncle Tom's Cabin is a book of extremes: the characters are either superhumanly noble or inhumanly cruel. None shows the common combination of human virtues and frailties. Uncle Tom is a black paragon; Simon Legree, his master, is an animal. Despite its lack of literary value, the work drove home some basic truths about the evils of this "peculiar institution." It was a powerful propaganda piece. Few readers could fail to weep with Uncle Tom when Legree sneered:

"Well here's a pious dog, at last, let down among us sinners!—a saint, a gentleman, and no less, to talk to us sinners
about our sins! Powerful holy crittur, he must be! Here, you
rascal, you make believe to be so pious,—didn't you never
hear out of yer Bible, Servant, obey yer master. An't I yer
master? Didn't I pay down twelve hundred dollars, cash, for
all there is inside yer cussed black shell? An't yer mine, now,
body and soul? . . ."

In the very depth of physical suffering, bowed by brutal
oppression, this question shot a gleam of joy and triumph
through Tom's soul. He suddenly stretched himself up, and,
looking earnestly to heaven, while the tears and blood that
flowed down his face mingled, he exclaimed,—

"No! no! no! my soul an't yours, Mas'r! You haven't
bought it,—ye can't buy it! It's been bought and paid for, by
one that is able to keep it;—no matter, no matter, you can't
harm me!"

It was Harriet Beecher Stowe who enlisted thousands of New England ministers in signing a petition two hundred feet long against the Kansas-
Nebraska Act. It was she who demanded, "Shall the
whole power of these United States go into the hands
of slavery?" By her book (and its many dramatizations
written by others), she aroused the conscience of
millions of Americans. Until they read or saw *Uncle
Tom's Cabin*, they had been content with the idea that

slavery was a necessary evil that would gradually disappear of its own volition.

Another result of the renewed resentment against the Fugitive Slave Law was the intensified activity of the Underground Railroad. Making little use of actual railroad lines, the Underground Railroad was a loose organization of people, black and white, who devoted themselves to smuggling slaves into safety in the free Northern states, in Canada, and even Mexico.

Slaves had always escaped whenever they could. And there were often a few people here and there who were ready to give the runaways a lift along the path to freedom. At first most of such help could be found in Pennsylvania and New Jersey. Later it became available all along the border between slave and free states. And when the first steam railroads came into general use in 1831, the Underground Railroad got its name. To continue the analogy, those who escorted the slaves along the way were known as "conductors," hiding places were "stations," and those who provided the hiding places were "stationmasters."

Most of the flights to freedom took place at night. By day the runaways hid and rested in one of the stations before starting on the next stage of their perilous journey. When night came, the slaves and their conductor emerged and again hurried north, guided by the stars and by landmarks familiar to the conductor. The best stations were barns on isolated farms and attics in country houses.

Sometimes conductors were able to provide the black fugitives with a vehicle—a covered wagon, a wagon with a closed compartment, or a closed carriage. Sometimes a runaway was even sealed into a large wooden box and shipped as freight by train or riverboat.

Who paid the expenses of these flights? The slaves had no money, so it was up to the whites to supply the vital funds. The Quakers (Friends) were especially helpful in raising money, as well as serving as conductors and stationmasters.

It was more or less to be expected that there would be antislavery whites in the North who would be active in the Underground Railroad, but there were also a surprising number of Southerners. Some at the risk of their lives offered the use of their farms or homes as stations. Others acted as conductors, especially in the danger-filled business of helping the fugitives across the Ohio River into freedom. Some Southern conductors actually posed as slave traders who were bringing blacks to auction or to their new owners.

Many Negroes worked for years on the Underground Railroad. Once slaves themselves, they returned again and again to the Deep South to lead fugitives to freedom. Sometimes a black conductor was caught and imprisoned or sold as a slave. Many, however, made good their second escape. Defying old and new masters, they returned to their dangerous trade.

One of the most famous black conductors on the Underground Railroad was Harriet Tubman. After escaping herself to the North, she returned South nineteen times and brought back at least three hundred slaves. Among those she led to freedom were her own mother, father, and sister.

Mrs. Tubman took no backtalk from any of her fugitives and was ready to abandon anyone who faltered or lagged along the way. One of her stratagems was to start for the North on a Saturday night. No printing was done on Sunday, so it would be Monday before newspaper advertisements or handbills telling of the runaways could appear.

After the Fugitive Slave Law of 1850 went into effect, Mrs. Tubman took her Underground Railroad passengers directly to Canada. No longer, she said, could she trust the United States government, even in the North, with her fugitives.

The Compromise of 1850—of which the Fugitive

Slave Law was a part—had been intended to smooth things over, to calm both the South and North. But the Kansas-Nebraska Act of 1854 only revived old injuries and injustices, and brought new ones. And when Kansas actually began to receive settlers, the people of the United States, both North and South, traveled even more swiftly down the road to Sumter.

The new settlers found rich farmland in eastern Kansas, well-watered and with good stretches of timber. In the western part of the territory they saw ample grazing areas, rising to uplands that approached the foothills of the Rocky Mountains. North of Kansas was the territory of Nebraska, perhaps less fertile and with harsher winters but good country, nonetheless.

Would these territories choose to be free or slave? That was the question in the nation's mind when the Kansas-Nebraska Act opened the land to settlement. Observers guessed that Nebraska would attract few slaveholding settlers. The usual slave-labor crops— cotton, hemp, tobacco—require a hot climate. They would not thrive on Nebraska's windswept prairies, more suitable for growing wheat and grazing cattle.

No, Nebraska was pretty sure to be free. But what about Kansas?

Kansas lay in the same zone of latitude as did much

of Illinois, Indiana, and Ohio—all free states. Geographically Kansas was not southern, and its crops would be temperate-zone farm products. But Kansas also lay just west of much of Missouri, and Missouri had entered the Union in 1820 as a slave state. Missouri was already bounded on the north and east by the free states of Iowa and Illinois. If Kansas were to be free as well, Missouri would be hemmed in by "enemies" to its slave-owning way of life.

So, in 1854, Missouri men were eager to push slavery into the new territory just west of their home state. "We are playing for a mighty stake," said Senator David Rice Atchison of Missouri. "If we win we carry slavery to the Pacific Ocean. If we fail we lose Missouri, Arkansas, Texas, and all the territories. The game must be played boldly."

In Kansas the Missouri men soon set up their little towns of Atchison (named for the senator) and Leavenworth (named for the army officer who had founded the fort nearby). These were located along the Missouri River where it forms the northeast border between Kansas and Missouri. The Free-Soilers—antislavery settlers—established the towns of Topeka and Lawrence along the Kansas (Kaw) River.

Almost at once the two factions were taking potshots

at each other. The principal issue was who owned the choice farm acreages that lay between their pairs of towns. The Free-Soilers were using their new Sharps rifles. These were nicknamed "Beecher's Bibles," after the Reverend Henry Ward Beecher, the brother of Harriet Beecher Stowe, and his remark that such rifles could be a "greater moral agency" than Bibles in Kansas.

The Kansas-Nebraska Act had been written so hastily that it neglected to say how long a person needed to live in the territories before he was eligible to vote. With no residency requirements for voting, Missouri men flooded into Kansas on election day and voted for a proslavery territorial delegate to Congress. Then "the voters" went back home. Later these same men elected a whole proslavery legislature. The Free-Soilers could not swallow such outright election frauds. They drew up their own constitution and elected their own legislature.

Missourians had taken such illegal measures because they were running scared. They had fifty thousand slaves, representing an investment of millions of dollars, in the western part of their state alone. They did not want to run the risk of slavery being abolished by Free-Soilers who claimed to be guided by a "higher law." But they needed help, so they tried to rally other slave states to their cause. For example, the Lafayette (Missouri) Emigration Society issued an appeal that said:

. . . Up to this time the border counties of Missouri have upheld and maintained the rights and interests of the South in this struggle, unassisted and unsuccessfully. But the Abolitionists, staking their all upon the Kansas issue . . . are moving heaven and earth to render that beautiful territory not only a free state, so-called, but a den of Negro thieves and "higher law" incendiaries.

Missouri . . . has done her duty . . . for the maintenance of the integrity of the South. But the time has come when she can no longer stand, single-handed, the lone champion of the South, against the myrmidons of the entire North. It requires no great foresight to perceive that if the "higher law" men succeed in this crusade, it will be but the commencement of a war upon the institutions of the South, which will continue until slavery shall cease to exist in any of the states or the Union is dissolved.

How, then, shall these impending evils be avoided? The answer is obvious. *Settle the territory with emigrants from the South. . . .*

The Emigration Society was calling for Southerners to move north. Some slaveowners responded to such appeals. But Kansas was really northern geographically, and most Deep Southerners knew it. Committed to slavery as they were, few were willing to attempt to transplant their plantation way of life to an area where the winters were sharp and cold. The Louisianians who had originally come north to settle central Missouri had given the name "Little Dixie" to their area. Kansas, however, did not inspire another "Little Dixie" settlement.

What did inspire Southerners to action were the slashing, intemperate verbal attacks made on them by Northern abolitionists. Many slaveowners were not Simon Legree types, crude and cruel. Many, especially the wealthy planters, were well educated, soft spoken, even courtly in their conduct. But attacks on slavery, the basis for their fortunes, could rouse them to fury. One such attack was made by Senator Charles Sumner of Massachusetts in a speech on the Senate floor:

. . . Sir, the Nebraska Bill was a swindle. It was a swindle by the South of the North. It was, on the part of those who had already completely enjoyed their share of the Missouri Compromise, a swindle of those whose share was yet absolutely untouched; and the plea of unconstitutionality set up—like the plea of usury after the borrowed money has been enjoyed —did not make it less a swindle. Urged as a bill of peace, it was a swindle of the whole country. Urged as opening the doors to slave masters with their slaves, it was a swindle of the asserted doctrine of popular sovereignty. Urged as sanctioning popular sovereignty, it was a swindle of the asserted rights of slave masters. It was a swindle of a broad territory, thus cheated of protection against slavery. It was the swindle of a great cause, early espoused by Washington, Franklin, and Jefferson, surrounded by the best fathers of the republic. Sir, it was a swindle of God-given inalienable rights. Turn it over; look at it on all sides, and it is everywhere a swindle. . . . No other word will adequately express the mingled meanness and wickedness of the cheat. . . .

Sumner then went on to make a bitter personal attack on Senator Andrew P. Butler of South Carolina, who was not present to speak in his own defense. Congressman Preston Brooks, also of South Carolina and a cousin of Senator Butler's, was incensed by Sumner's tirade. Two days later, armed with a cane, he attacked Sumner in the Senate chamber without warning and gave him a vicious beating. Southern newspapers hailed Brooks as a hero, and admirers presented him with canes inscribed with their warmest sentiments. Sumner did not completely recover from the beating for years.

John Brown
and Dred Scott

ONLY a few days after Charles Sumner was beaten on the Senate floor, a gang of Missouri "border ruffians" swooped down on Lawrence, Kansas, where the Free-Soilers had set up their territorial capital. They set fire to several buildings and wrecked the newspaper office and printing shop. For this, a grim, gray-bearded, fanatical abolitionist named John Brown took a terrible revenge.

Brown, accompanied by four of his sons, a son-in-law, and two others, bullied his way into a small pro-slavery settlement on Pottawatomie Creek on the night of May 24, 1856. In retaliation for the raid on Lawrence, they dragged five men out of their homes and murdered them, hacking away at their bodies with sabers. None of the victims actually owned slaves, and two were German-born, with no ties at all to the South.

John Brown, "God's angry man," may actually have been insane. Nevertheless he was able to infect many others with his religious zeal and righteousness. Born in Connecticut in 1800, he came from a family who considered it their Christian duty to fight against slavery. During his boyhood he lived in Ohio, and as a young man he did not drink, dance, or play cards. He would not even hunt or fish, because these were "lazy" habits.

Brown married young, and when his first wife died, he married again. By his two wives he had a total of twenty children. Brown worked hard as a farmer and businessman, but he was always in debt, always being sued.

For years Brown thought that the South would eventually see the light and give up slavery of its own free will. But in 1837 the murder of Elijah Lovejoy radicalized Brown. The mob slaying made him realize that the South would never willingly give up the moneymaking practice of keeping the blacks enslaved. He saw too that abolishing the practice would require a bloody battle. Brown was now ready to throw himself into, even lead, that battle.

Soon Brown conjured up a mad scheme. He would

John Brown

march at the head of his own army into the South, going from plantation to plantation and freeing the blacks. He cherished this scheme for years, talking it over with his fellow white abolitionists and with such black leaders as Frederick Douglass. He even got Gerrit Smith, a rich antislavery man, who lived in up-state New York, to give him part of a huge tract of land in the Adirondack Mountains. There Smith planned to settle the blacks Brown would have brought to freedom.

When the Fugitive Slave Law of 1850 was passed, Brown actually exulted. He wrote his wife: "It now seems that the Fugitive Slave Law was to be the means of making more Abolitionists than all the lectures we have had for years. It really looks as if God had his hand in this wickedness also." He was perfectly sincere in his reference to the deity.

For years Brown continued to prepare himself for his great crusade. He studied texts by military strategists and maps of the areas he planned to invade. Before Brown himself went to Kansas, however, he sent five of his sons ahead. They were soon caught up in the fights between the Free-Soilers and proslavers. In time Brown joined his sons, ready to lead the crusade. He struck his first blow at Pottawatomie Creek, shocking the Free-Soilers with the savage murders and spurring the border ruffians to further destruction. The proslavers conducted a manhunt for Brown, but without success. They did find two of his sons and put them to death, even though these particular young men had not taken part in the Pottawatomie massacre.

Undiscouraged, Brown renewed the assault. He raided the proslavery settlements for horses and supplies and took on the border ruffians in brief skirmishes. That summer of 1856 in Osawatomie, Kansas, he earned a reputation as a commander, and a grim nickname as well. With a band of about forty abolitionists he fought off an attack by a company of proslavers six times as large. Brown's son Frederick was slain, and his men were forced to retreat, but not before they had done considerable damage to their foes. Thenceforth old John was known as "Osawatomie" Brown.

A week after the Pottawatomie slayings, but completely unconnected with them, there came the chance for Abraham Lincoln to win a national reputation. The date was May 29, 1856; the place was Bloomington, Illinois; and the occasion was a convention of Illinois newspaper editors who opposed the Kansas-Nebraska Act. The principal convention speaker was Lincoln, a private citizen but a prime mover and shaker of public political opinion.

Lincoln delivered a long, emotion-packed address, perhaps one of the greatest in his career. But every member of his audience, most of them trained reporters, was too swept up and away to take any notes. And Lincoln had not made a draft of it or even jotted down an outline. Thus the speech was irretrievably lost, except in the fading memories of those who had listened to it.

One man in the audience, Henry C. Whitney, however, claimed to have remembered the speech just as it was delivered. In its issue of September 1896—forty years after Lincoln spoke—*McClure's Magazine* published what was allegedly a word-for-word transcript of the speech—as set down from memory by Whitney.

But only two sentences of Whitney's version stood up in a cross-checking with the recollections of others who had heard Lincoln that day. The first sentence dealt with a threat uttered by some Northerners to invade Kansas "with Sharp's rifles." Nearly everyone agreed that Lincoln had said: "No, my friends, I'll tell you what we'll do. We'll wait until November [referring to the forthcoming presidential election of 1856], and then we'll shoot paper ballots at them."

This first was a relatively minor quotation. The second remembered line came at the close of his speech, more than an hour later. The end-of-May twilight was deepening, but the lamps had not yet been lit in the hall. The eyes of more than a thousand people in the audience were fixed on the face of the speaker, on his clenched, pounding fists. They were hypnotized by his high-pitched but powerful voice as he said:

"We say to our Southern brethren, 'We *won't* go out of the Union, and you SHAN'T!'"

It was a rousing climax to his long address. And nearly everyone who was questioned years later agreed that Lincoln, except for a concluding sentence or two, ended on this precise note. It was, by all accounts, a magnificent performance. Who knows what effect the speech might have had if it could have been published in newspapers across the nation?

More than a hint of what the Bloomington speech might have contained was in an address Lincoln delivered at Kalamazoo, Michigan, three months later. Fortunately this text has been preserved. The audience in Kalamazoo was largely made up of Northern Democrats. Lincoln—a Whig, shortly to become a Republican—appealed to them on their own party principles.

After describing the United States as a vital, prosperous "empire," he went on to discuss slavery in dollars-and-cents terms. "The estimated worth of the slaves in the South is $1,000,000,000, and in a very few years, if the institution shall be admitted into the territories, they will have increased fifty per cent in value." How to stop the spread of slavery? By sticking to the Constitution, Lincoln said.

Lincoln called on the Democrats to "come forward . . . come to the rescue of this great principle of equality. Don't interfere with anything in the Constitution. . . . Come, and keep coming! Strike, and strike again! . . ."

Yet many of the Northern Democrats were in sympathy with their Southern political allies and with their belief in popular sovereignty. Lincoln's speech was coolly received. And for the moment the Democrats held the winning political cards in the presidential race. They elected James Buchanan, defeating the candidate of the new Republican party, John C. Frémont.

Buchanan was inaugurated on March 4, 1857. Two days after Buchanan was sworn in, the Supreme Court announced its momentous Dred Scott decision.

Dred Scott was a black who had been the slave of Dr. John Emerson, an army surgeon who lived in Missouri, where slavery was legal. In 1834, twenty-three years before the Supreme Court finally reviewed Scott's plea, Dr. Emerson had taken Scott with him to

Illinois and later to a part of the Wisconsin Territory. Slavery was banned in the territory by the Missouri Compromise of 1820. In time Emerson took Scott back to Missouri. Then Emerson died, and Scott was sold to a man named Sanford (or Sandford).

Some interested observers, wanting to see justice done, advised Scott that his residence in a state and territory where slavery was illegal had made him a free man. Scott thereupon sued Mrs. Emerson for his freedom in 1846. The state circuit court ruled in his favor, but the state supreme court upset the lower court's decision. Scott (and his backers) then took the case to the federal courts. For eleven years the suit moved up and up, from one court to the next, until at last it reached the United States Supreme Court.

Chief Justice Roger Brooke Taney was a confirmed Maryland slaveowner. He and the four other Southerners on the Supreme Court bench saw in the Dred Scott case their chance to extend slavery through all the territories. Here was their reasoning:

1. As a black, Scott was not a citizen of the United States and thus had no right to bring suit in a federal court.
2. Since he was at present a resident of the slave

Dred Scott

Chief Justice
Roger Taney

state of Missouri—to which he had returned without protest—the laws of Illinois had no longer any bearing on whether Scott was slave or free.

3. Simply living in the free Wisconsin Territory had also not set Scott free, because Congress had no right to deprive United States citizens (Emerson or Sanford) of their property (the slave, Scott) without due process of law.

4. Therefore, the Supreme Court concluded, slavery

could not be prohibited in territories north of
36° 30′—the line of the Missouri Compromise.

The logic of the Court had a dual result. It had
ruled both that it had no *jurisdiction* (authority) in
the Dred Scott case and that the Missouri Compromise
was unconstitutional.

The Supreme Court's decision roused fury in the
North, especially among the abolitionists and Republicans. They charged that it would, in effect, make
slavery legal everywhere. If a slaveowner could not be
deprived of his slaves by living in a free territory, why
couldn't he keep them in a free state as well? William
Lloyd Garrison cried out: "No Union with slaveholders!" For his part, Wendell Phillips branded the
Union as "accursed of God—away with it!"

Even Stephen Douglas and the Northern Democrats
were shaken by the Dred Scott verdict. If settlers in a
new territory wanted to keep slavery out but were
unable to do so, what did popular sovereignty mean?
Once it had meant that the settlers were free to choose.
But if slavery was already legal, there was no choice.

But Douglas soon convinced himself and his fol-
lowers that popular sovereignty was not really threatened by the Supreme Court's decision. A slaveowner,

Douglas argued, couldn't bring slaves into a territory unless his action was "sustained, protected, and enforced by appropriate police regulations and local legislation." In other words, people in a territory could keep slavery out by denying it the protection of territorial laws.

In siding with Chief Justice Taney, Douglas also took a dig at Abraham Lincoln. "All men are created equal," as stated in the Declaration of Independence, did not include blacks—so asserted Douglas. Such an equalitarian view, he continued, meant in the end that blacks in the United States had every political, economic, and social right that whites had. And this included the right to marry a white mate.

In his only political speech of 1857 Lincoln answered Douglas' charges. Speaking at Springfield on June 26, Lincoln maintained that the Supreme Court had been clearly wrong in its Dred Scott decision and was bound to reverse itself sooner or later. Meantime the Court's verdict must be respected and obeyed.

As for all men being created equal, Lincoln argued that they were surely not equal in every way. And in saying that he did not want a black woman as a slave, he was not implying that he wanted to marry her. "In some respects she certainly is not my equal," he said, "but in her natural right to eat the bread she earns with her own hands without asking leave of any one else, she is my equal, and the equal of all others."

Lincoln had arrived at about his most mature position regarding black equality. Today some people brand that position as racist. It may be true that such a statement offered today would be looked on as less than liberal. But in the 1850's it was advanced, even radical. Lincoln was well ahead of his times.

ELEVEN

The Debates, Then Harpers Ferry

IN 1858 Abraham Lincoln became the Republican candidate for the office of United States senator from Illinois. This time his Democratic opponent was none other than Stephen A. Douglas, now running for re-election. Lincoln was also, in a sense, running against the pushers of illegal, semilegal, and extralegal measures that would either install slavery in every state and territory in the Union—or split the nation in two.

Lincoln launched his campaign at the Republican state convention which met in Springfield in June 1858. On June 16 the convention unanimously approved this resolution: "Resolved, that Abraham Lincoln is the first and only choice of the Republicans of

Illinois for the United States Senate, as the successor of Stephen A. Douglas."

That night Lincoln gave the first speech of his campaign. Although it was not widely reprinted, his talk nevertheless caught the attention of alert students of politics all across the country—and it added to Lincoln's growing stature as a statesman and political thinker. He began by saying:

If we could first know where we are and whither we are tending, we could better judge what to do and how to do it. We are now far into the fifth year since a policy was initiated with the avowed object and confident promise of putting an end to slavery agitation. Under the operation of that policy, the agitation has not only not ceased but has constantly augmented. In my opinion, it will not cease until a crisis shall have been reached and passed.

A house divided against itself cannot stand. I believe this government cannot endure, permanently, half slave and half free. I do not expect the Union to be dissolved—I do not expect the house to fall—but I do expect it will cease to be divided. It will become all one thing or all the other.

Either the opponents of slavery will arrest the further spread of it, and place it where the public mind shall rest in the belief that it is in the course of ultimate extinction, or its advocates will push it forward, till it shall become alike lawful in all the states, old as well as new—North as well as South.

The second alternative, Lincoln was suggesting, was simply unacceptable. He followed this with a sharp analysis of the Kansas-Nebraska Act and the Dred Scott decision. Freedom would become a lost cause, he pointed out, if the law's protection was to be further chipped away by such actions of Congress and the Supreme Court.

Douglas answered by first denying Lincoln's charges. "I regard the great principle of popular sovereignty as having been made triumphant in this land," he said, "as a permanent rule of public policy in the organization of territories and the admission of states. . . ." Popular sovereignty would not "divide the house"; it would make the house even stronger.

But Lincoln, so Douglas charged, was actually fomenting a civil war, a war between the states. He was inviting the free states to band together and attack the slave states. And in the same breath Lincoln was notifying the slave states "to stand together as a unit and make an aggressive war upon the free states of the Union with a view of establishing slavery in them all. . . ."

And all this, asserted Douglas, for the sake of "uniformity." Lincoln "goes for uniformity in our domestic institutions, for a war of sections, until one or the other shall be subdued. I go for the great principle of the

Kansas-Nebraska Bill—the right of the people to decide for themselves."

Lincoln certainly wanted to win the Senate seat from Douglas. But he wanted even more—he wanted to defeat and destroy the whole idea of popular sovereignty. It was an idea, he knew, that would lead only to the extension of slavery and ultimately wreck the Union.

So Lincoln challenged Douglas to a series of seven debates, to be held in various Illinois towns. The first would take place in Ottawa on August 21, 1858; the last at Alton on October 15. In between, there would be encounters at Freeport, Jonesboro, Charleston, Galesburg (where Carl Sandburg, Lincoln's noted biographer, would be born in 1878), and Quincy, on the Mississippi, just upriver from Mark Twain's Hannibal, Missouri. Douglas accepted the challenge.

The Lincoln-Douglas debates turned out to be the most important verbal duels in American history. They attracted vast throngs of listeners; country people hitched up their buggies and drove miles into town to hear the two candidates speak. In the days before radio and television brought politicians into the living room, many voters were willing to travel long distances to hear vote-getting speeches.

The talks loosely followed the form of a conven-

tional debate, with pro and con sides taken on a question and each speaker allowed rebuttal to the major arguments of the other. Unlike a conventional debate, however, there was no appointed judge and no announced winner. In one sense it may be said that Lincoln lost the contest, for Douglas was reelected to the Senate in November. But in defining the issues in 1858, Lincoln won the attention of the new Republican party—and in 1860 went on to win the presidential election.

At the opening debate in Ottawa, Douglas flatly declared that he was opposed to granting citizenship to the blacks. But Lincoln, he claimed, believed that "the Negro was made his equal and hence his brother." And he again attacked Lincoln for his stand on "uniformity" —a nation uniformly free or uniformly slave. Why couldn't the United States go on as before, with some states free and some slave?

Lincoln denied that he wanted "to interfere with the institution of slavery in the states where it existed." Nor did he want "political and social equality" between blacks and whites. But the Negro was fully entitled to the basic rights called for in the Declaration of Independence—life, liberty, and the pursuit of happiness. On this he stood firm.

At the second meeting Lincoln trapped Douglas into a damaging admission. He posed this question: Can the people of a territory keep slavery out? Under Douglas' popular sovereignty view, the answer should be "yes." But the Supreme Court's Dred Scott decision said that Congress had no power to keep slavery out of a territory. According to this, the answer should be "no."

By answering "yes," Douglas would anger the South. A "no" answer would displease the North. Douglas came up with the position he had taken before. He said that slavery could not exist in a territory, no matter what the Supreme Court had said, unless it had the support of local police regulations. A territory could exclude slavery by "unfriendly legislation."

Douglas' answer became known as the Freeport doctrine, after the town where the second debate took place. It was clever enough to win him the Senate election in 1858. But it split his own Democratic party right down the national middle. In 1860 Douglas was nominated for the Presidency by the Northern Democrats. The Southern Democrats refused to consider him their candidate. Without the support of his party's Southern wing, Douglas could not win the election.

In the remaining debates, Lincoln slashed away at

Douglas' Freeport doctrine and exposed its fallacies. In the last debate, at Alton, Lincoln referred to the fact that the Constitution nowhere uses the words "Negro" or "slavery." He contended that the Constitution-makers ardently hoped that one day slavery would vanish from the American scene.

Finally Lincoln brought Douglas back to consider what Lincoln's position in the debates had been all along. Lincoln was not fighting the right of *existing states* to be slave, if that was their choice. What Lincoln was fighting was the extension of slavery into the *new territories*.

All through the debates Lincoln had been defining and limiting his positions with a lawyer's precise caution. He knew that slavery was morally wrong, and had said so. But it was legal in the states which had decreed it so, and Lincoln was not willing to go beyond the limits of the law. Yet his idea of those same limits was ready to be expanded.

Reports of the Lincoln-Douglas debates were published in papers all over the United States. Many Americans heard of Abraham Lincoln for the first time, and many (mainly in the North) liked what they heard. They respected his clear expression and logical thought, uncluttered by emotion; they were eager to know more about him.

But the forces of fanaticism were also on the rise. After Osawatomie, John Brown made several trips East to collect money and guns for his crusade. Shuttling between Kansas and the seaboard cities, he was sick and weak, but his eyes glittered with the intensity of his mission. For now Brown had definite plans for his crusade. He would capture the town of Harpers Ferry, Virginia, seize its federal arsenal, and distribute its arms

to all the blacks and antislavery whites who were sure to rally round at the news, then lead this army south until every slave was freed.

With a force of eighteen men—thirteen white and five black—Brown struck at Harpers Ferry on the night of October 16, 1859. By dawn he had taken the town and the arsenal. But the Virginia Guard and a detachment of federal troops under Colonel Robert E. Lee soon struck back. Several of Brown's men were killed; some escaped; and Brown and four others were taken prisoner.

As they had done after Nat Turner's revolt three decades before, the whole South shuddered at the thought that Brown might have been successful. Within a week Brown was brought to trial. Too sick to walk, he was carried into court on a cot. He was soon found guilty and sentenced to be hanged. Hearing the verdict, he mustered enough strength to stand and address the court:

In the first place I deny everything but what I have all along admitted: the design on my part to free slaves . . . had I so interfered in behalf of the rich, the powerful, the intelligent, the so-called great . . . and suffered and sacrificed what I have in this interference, it would have been all right, and every man in this court would have deemed it an act worthy of reward rather than punishment.

. . . the Bible . . . teaches me that all things whatsoever I would that men should do to me, I should do even so to them. It teaches me, further, to "remember them that are in bonds, as bound with them." . . . Now, if it is deemed necessary that I should forfeit my life for the furtherance of the ends of justice and mingle my blood further with the blood of my children and with the blood of millions in this slave country whose rights are disregarded by wicked, cruel, and unjust enactments, I submit; so let it be done! . . .

This was not John Brown's last word. On December 2, 1859, the day of the execution, he handed one of his guards a note as he left his cell. It read:

I, John Brown, am now quite *certain* that the crimes of this *guilty land*: *will* never be purged *away*; but with Blood. I had *as* I *now think*: *vainly* flattered myself that without *very much* bloodshed it might be done.

Brown was correctly sensing the coming conflict. He saw the road leading up to Sumter.

As Brown's lifeless body hung on the scaffold, the officer in charge pronounced what he thought was the final judgment on the old man's career: "So perish all such enemies of Virginia! All such enemies of the Union! All such foes of the human race!"

But in the Civil War that was to commence a brief fifteen months later, Union soldiers rendered a different judgment as they sang:

> *John Brown's body lies a-moulderin' in the grave,*
> *His soul goes marching on!*

Road to Sumter, Road to War

Two MONTHS after the execution of John Brown, Lincoln was about to journey to New Hampshire to visit his eldest son, Robert, a student at Phillips Exeter Academy. Noting that he would be in the vicinity, the Plymouth Church in Brooklyn, New York, invited him to speak from its pulpit. (The pastor of the church was the same Henry Ward Beecher after whom the "Beecher's Bibles" were named.) The lecture fee would be two hundred dollars, and Lincoln was free to choose his own topic.

The Republican national convention was then only several months away, and no prime presidential prospect had yet come forward. One of the party's kingmakers was William Cullen Bryant, editor of the New York *Evening Post* (and a popular poet as well). He wanted to see how well Lincoln, whom he admired for his showing in the 1858 Lincoln-Douglas debates, would fare before a sophisticated Eastern audience. If Lincoln could sell himself to these listeners, Bryant thought, he might very well become the Republican standard-bearer.

So Bryant used his friends and his influence to have Lincoln's address moved from the Brooklyn church to Manhattan, to the Great Hall of the new Cooper Union for the Advancement of Science and Art. The Great Hall was, at the time, the biggest and fanciest auditorium in the United States. If Abraham Lincoln could hold his audience in the Great Hall, he could hold one anywhere in the world.

Lincoln arrived in New York City on Saturday, February 25, 1860. He went directly to the Astor House, on already-famed Broadway, and worked on his speech all day. On Sunday morning he went to hear Henry Ward Beecher preach in his Brooklyn church. On Monday the Republican reception committee escorted Lincoln to the photography studio of Mathew B. Brady. There Lincoln sat before Brady's portrait camera, and photographic history was made.

Photography had been in existence for only a few

decades, but Brady's technique would rival that of many modern masters. He captured on his wet-plate negatives Lincoln's great humanity and brooding sorrow. In the deep-set eyes and strongly lined features of his subject (Lincoln did not grow a beard until he became President), Brady found—and photographed —Lincoln's true self.

That evening Abraham Lincoln faced a great test. Facing an audience of fifteen hundred fashionable men and women, he started slowly and nervously, his voice faltering and cracking. The audience was inclined to snicker—this Illinois countryman looked so awkward and ill at ease, with his gaunt face, his lanky frame, and his ill-fitting clothes. But Lincoln had done his homework well, and the carefully prepared Cooper Union speech was one of his very best. At the outset he answered Douglas' charge that the nation's Founding Fathers, "when they framed the government under which we live, understood this question just as well, and even better than we do now." And "this question," as Lincoln saw it, was: "Does the proper division of local from federal authority, or anything in the Constitution, forbid our federal government to control . . . slavery in our federal territories?"

Patiently Lincoln demonstrated that the vast majority of the framers of the Constitution had voted for federal control over slavery in the territories every time the issue was raised in Congress—and it had come up many times in the first several Congresses. So much for Douglas' charge that the Founding Fathers were inclined to favor, or at least to tolerate, slavery. As for the present Republican position on slavery, it was simply this: ". . . an evil not to be extended but to be tolerated and protected only because . . . its actual presence among us makes that toleration and protection a necessity."

He denied that the Republicans had encouraged John Brown's raid on Harpers Ferry. And he scoffed at the allegation that the Republican party had aided Nat Turner's revolt three decades before. As a party, the Republicans were less than four years old.

Lincoln closed his Cooper Union address with a poetic and eloquent statement: "Neither let us be slandered from our duty by false accusations against us, nor frightened from it by menaces of destruction to the government, nor of dungeons to ourselves. Let us have faith that right makes might, and in that faith let us, to the end, dare to do our duty as we understand it."

Three months later Lincoln won the Republican presidential nomination. Recalling his photographs and his landmark speech, he said fondly, "Brady and the Cooper Union made me President." The statement was, of course, a deliberate oversimplification. It was time for Lincoln to capture the nomination and the election, and nothing could stand in his way.

In mid-May of 1860 delegates by the thousand descended on Chicago for the Republican national convention. Illinois Republicans had met in Decatur the previous week and had unanimously chosen Lincoln as their man. Lincoln, as both he and his backers well knew, faced formidable opposition. There was Senator William H. Seward of New York, who was considered more of a radical on the slavery question than Lincoln. There was Salmon P. Chase of Ohio, who was even more of an abolitionist than Seward. There were several other contenders.

The convention met in the Wigwam, a rambling wooden building in the center of town, erected just for the convention. Lincoln's campaign managers set up shop in the nearby Tremont House. (Neither structure still stands.) Under their chief strategist, Judge David Davis of Bloomington, they moved to secure the nomination for their candidate. Meanwhile Lincoln himself remained at home in Springfield.

The majority needed to gain the nomination was

233 votes. On the first ballot it was Seward 173½, Lincoln 102, with Chase and the others trailing far behind. Lincoln gained 79 votes on the second ballot, but Seward advanced by only eleven. The third round was to be the critical one.

Lincoln's count mounted steadily. It reached 231½ —and two more would make him the winner. At that point newspaper publisher Joseph Medill, one of Lincoln's campaign staff, whispered into the ear of David Cartter, Chase's Ohio leader: "If you can throw the Ohio delegation to Lincoln, Chase can have anything he wants." Cartter immediately announced the switch of four votes from Chase to Lincoln. It was, as they say, all over except the shouting.

(Medill's promise was kept. Chase became Secretary of the Treasury, and Seward, Lincoln's chief rival for the nomination, was appointed Secretary of State.)

The plank in the Republican party platform on slavery was somewhat mediocre. It demanded that Kansas be admitted only as a free state, hooted at popular sovereignty, and charged that any relegalization of the importing of slaves would be an outright crime. But on the matter of slavery in the new territories, it merely denied the right of Congress or a territorial legislature to permit the practice in a territory.

Douglas was Lincoln's principal opponent in the 1860 presidential race. But there were two other candidates, John C. Breckinridge on the Southern Democratic ticket and John Bell of the hastily formed National Constitutional Union party, who were also running primarily against Lincoln. The odds favored Lincoln because the other three contenders might split the anti-Republican vote. Lincoln gathered 1,866,452 popular votes and 180 electoral votes—and won by a wide electoral margin.

Election Day was November 6, 1860; Inauguration Day was not until the following March 4. During those four months Lincoln tried to make peace with the South. One North Carolina statesman wrote: "He [Lincoln] is regarded as neither a dangerous or a bad man. We have no fears that he is going to attempt any great outrage upon us. We rather suppose his purpose will be to conciliate. But it is . . . the *fundamental idea* that underlies the whole movement of his nomination and . . . his election. It is the declaration of unceasing war against slavery as an institution." Other Southerners, privately and in print, denounced Lincoln in strongly personal terms. And one by one the Southern states spurned his peace offerings.

South Carolina, as we have seen, was the first state

to secede. It was soon followed by Mississippi, Florida, Alabama, Georgia, and Louisiana. On February 1, 1861, Texas seceded, completing the roster of Gulf states. The Confederate States of America then commandeered the federal forts (except for Sumter), arsenals, customs offices, and other federal installations within their borders.

But other Southern states did not seem ready to secede. Virginia, whose voice was respected in the South, chose 122 pro-Union men as against 30 secessionists as delegates to a special state convention to consider secession. The convention ruled that any movement toward secession must be affirmed by popular vote. Seven Southern states had seceded—but eight others seemed sure to stay in the Union. Could the Union survive such a loss?

President-elect Lincoln left Springfield on February 11, one day before his fifty-third birthday, for Washington, D.C. The winding railroad journey took twelve days, with receptions and speeches in the larger cities and back-platform appearances at the whistle stops.

On his way East, Lincoln received word that Jefferson Davis, once secretary of war, had been sworn in as president of the Confederate States of America. The seceding states had united and formed a government, ready to deal with the United States as a foreign country. The Confederacy was soon bidding for relations with European nations.

It was a discouraging and even frightening time for Lincoln. But he took heart as he stopped in Philadelphia to raise the flag at Independence Hall. "I have often inquired of myself," he said, "what great principle or idea it was that kept this [nation] so long together. It was not the mere matter of the separation of the colonies from the mother land, but that something in the Declaration [of Independence] giving liberty, not alone to the people of this country, but hope to the world for all future time. It was that which gave promise that in due time the weights should be lifted from the shoulders of all men, and that *all* should have an equal chance."

By *all*, Lincoln certainly included the blacks.

Because of a rumored assassination plot, Lincoln was persuaded to enter Washington secretly, his face half-hidden in a long winding scarf. And because of a fear of violence, his inauguration on March 4 was only sparsely attended. His inaugural address was both friendly and firm.

Lincoln began his speech by expressing his friendship towards the South, even to the new Confederacy:

Apprehension seems to exist among the people of the Southern states that, by the accession of a Republican administration, their property and their peace and personal security are
to be endangered. There has never been any reasonable
cause for such apprehension. Indeed, the most ample evidence to the contrary has all the while existed and been open
to their inspection.

But the Gulf states seceded illegally, argued the new
President, and the Union thus remained unbroken. "No
state, upon its own mere motion, can lawfully get out
of the Union." Therefore all he would do as President
would be "to hold, occupy, and possess the property
and places belonging to the government" in the seceded states. There would be "no invasion—no using
of force against or among the people anywhere."

Lincoln closed his speech with an eloquent plea for
peace and reconciliation:

In *your* hands, my dissatisfied fellow countrymen, and not in
mine, is the momentous issue of civil war. The government
will not assail *you*. You can have no conflict without your-
selves being the aggressors. *You* have no oath registered in
heaven to destroy the government, while *I* shall have the
most solemn one to "preserve, protect, and defend" it.

I am loath to close. We are not enemies but friends. We

must not be enemies. Though passion may have strained, it must not break, our bonds of affection. . . .

But the road to Sumter, as we have seen, had all but come to an end. Within weeks the most tragic of all wars, a war between brothers, would begin.

Bibliography

ADLER, MORTIMER, ed. The Annals of America, Volume 7, *1841–1849 Manifest Destiny*; Volume 8, *1850–1857 A House Dividing*; Volume 9, *1858–1865 The Crisis of the Union*. Encyclopaedia Britannica, 1968.

BENNETT, LERONE, JR. *Before the Mayflower: A History of Black America.* Johnson, 1969.

CANBY, COURTLAND, ed. *Lincoln and the Civil War.* Dell, 1958.

CARMAN, HARRY J.; SYRETT, HAROLD C.; WISHY, BERNARD W. *A History of the American People.* Knopf, 1964.

CATTON, BRUCE. *The Coming Fury.* Doubleday, 1961.

CRAVEN, AVERY. *The Coming of the Civil War.* Univ. of Chicago Press, 1957.

CRISSEY, ELWELL. *Lincoln's Lost Speech.* Hawthorn, 1967.

CURRENT, RICHARD N. *John C. Calhoun.* Washington Square Press, 1963.

DOUGLASS, FREDERICK. *Life and Times of Frederick Douglass.* Crowell-Collier, 1962.

DRIMMER, MELVIN, ed. *Black History.* Doubleday, 1968.

DUNAWAY, PHILIP, and DE KAY, GEORGE, eds. *Turning Point.* Random, 1958.

FRANKLIN, JOHN HOPE. *From Slavery to Freedom.* Knopf, 1967.

GRIERSON, FRANCIS. *The Valley of Shadows.* Harper, 1948.

HESSELTINE, WILLIAM B., ed. *Three Against Lincoln.* Louisiana State Univ. Press, 1960.

HOFSTADTER, RICHARD. *The American Political Tradition.* Knopf, 1948.

HOOVER, DWIGHT W., ed. *Understanding Negro History.* Quadrangle, 1968.

JAFFA, HARRY V. "Expediency and Morality in the Lincoln-Douglas Debates," *Anchor Review.* Doubleday, 1957.

JONES, PETER d'A. *The Consumer Society.* Pelican, 1965.

LANGFORD, MALCOLM S., JR. *The American Civil War.* Scholastic, 1968.

MADISON, CHARLES A. *Critics and Crusaders.* Holt, 1947–48.

MIRSKY, JEANNETTE, and NEVINS, ALLAN. *The World of Eli Whitney.* Macmillan, 1952.

MORISON, SAMUEL ELIOT. *The Oxford History of the American People.* Oxford, 1965.

NEWMAN, RALPH G., ed. *Lincoln for the Ages.* Doubleday, 1960.

RAWLEY, JAMES A. *Race and Politics.* Lippincott, 1969.

SANDBURG, CARL. *Abraham Lincoln: The Prairie Years and the War Years.* Harcourt, 1954.

SEABERG, STANLEY. *The Negro in American History.* Scholastic, 1968.

STERN, PHILIP VAN DOREN, ed. *Prologue to Sumter.* Indiana Univ. Press, 1963.

THOMAS, BENJAMIN P. *Abraham Lincoln.* Knopf, 1952.

Index

abolitionist(s), 61–75
  Abraham Lincoln as an, 76, 82–85
  John Brown as an, 130–133, 151–154
  Frederick Douglass as an, 76–80, 133
  newspapers of the, 64–68, 70, 79
  and slave trading in the District of Columbia, 97, 101
  William Lloyd Garrison as an, 64–77, 140
Adams, John Quincy:
  as President, 90, 91
  in House of Representatives, 98
  as Secretary of State, 89

Adirondack Mountains, 133
Africa, 23, 24, 34, 36, 46, 55, 62, 63
Alabama, secession of, 163
Alton, Ill., 82, 146, 150
American Anti-Slavery Society, 68–69
American Colonization Society, 62–63, 113
American party, see Know-Nothing party
American Revolution, 15, 37, 43, 83
  blacks in, 46
Anderson, Major Robert, 4, 6–9, 11
Arawak Indians, 35–36
Arizona, 105

Arkansas, 89
Ashley River, 4
Asia, 34
Atchison, David Rice, 125
Auld, Mrs. Hugh, 77
Austin, James T., 74

Bailey v. *Cromwell,* 84
Balboa, Vasco Núñez de, 35
Baltimore, Md., 66, 77
Beauregard, Pierre Gustave Toutant, 9, 10–11
Beecher, Henry Ward, 126, 155, 156
"Beecher's Bibles," 126
Bell, John, 126
Black Hawk War, 81
blacks (*see also* slave(s); slavery):
  bringing of, to America, 34–35, 37
  returning of, to Africa, 62–63
  uprisings by, 49–60
  white advocates of freedom for, 61–75
Bloomington, Ill., 134, 160
bondsmen:
  black, 36–37
  white, 36
Boston, Mass., 15, 41, 70, 71, 72
Brady, Mathew B., 156, 158, 160
Brazil, 35
Breckinridge, John C., 162
Brooklyn, N.Y., 155
Brooklyn, U.S.S., 7

Brooks, Preston, 129
Brown, John, 130–133, 155
  Harpers Ferry raid of, 151–154, 159
Bryant, William Cullen, 156
Buchanan, James, 7, 137
Burns, Anthony, 116
Butler, Andrew P., 129

Calhoun, John C.:
  as Senator, 96–102
  as Vice-President, 92–95
California, 99, 100, 107
  gold rush, 100
Canada, 50, 120, 122
Cartter, David, 161
Castle Pinckney, 4
Charleston, Ill, 146
Charleston, S.C., 3
  federal property in, 4–11
  uprising in, 52–55
Chase, Salmon P., 109, 159, 160, 161
Chew, Robert, 10
Chicago, Ill., 107, 160
Christianity, 31, 32, 63
Cibola, Seven Cities of, 35
Civil War, 11, 165–166
Clay, Henry, 62, 100–103
Cobb, Jeremiah, 59–60
Columbia, S.C., 2
Columbian Orator, The, 77
Columbus, Christopher, 35
Committee to Prepare an Ordinance of Secession, 3

Compromise of 1850, 100–103, 104
  Fugitive Slave Law of, 48, 100–103, 115–116, 120, 122–124, 133
Confederate States of America, formation of, 9, 163–164, 165–166
Congress, U.S.:
  "gag resolution" in, 97–99
  North-South political relationships in, 86–103
  slavery as an issue in, 2, 25, 48, 97–98, 159, 161
  tariff of abominations and, 90–96
Connecticut, 131
  abolition of slavery in, 46
Constitution, U.S., 3, 19, 25, 80, 86, 90, 97, 102, 137, 150, 158, 159
  Article I, Section 9, 47
  Article IV, Section 2, 48
  Thirteenth Amendment, 19, 48
  Fourteenth Amendment, 19
  Fifteenth Amendment, 19
  Seventeenth Amendment, 114
Constitutional Convention of 1787, 46–47
Continental Congress, 43–44
Cooper Union for the Advancement of Sciences and Art, Lincoln's speech at, 156, 158–159

Coronado, Francisco, 35
Cortés, Hernando, 35
cotton (see also plantations; slave(s); slavery):
  and the rolling gin, 17–18
  and Eli Whitney's gin, 18–20
cotton mills:
  in England, 13, 19
  in the North, 13, 19

Davis, David, 160
Davis, Jefferson:
  as President of the Confederate States of America, 9, 163
  as Secretary of War, 105, 108
Decatur, Ill., 160
Declaration of Independence, 43–44, 141, 148, 164
Democratic party, 110, 149
  Northern members of, 109, 136, 137, 140, 149
  Southern, 162
District of Columbia, slave trading in, 97, 101
Douglas, Stephen A., 140, 141, 143–146, 162
  and the Compromise of 1850, 100–103
  and the Kansas-Nebraska Act, 107–108, 111–114
  Freeport doctrine of, 149–150
  and the Lincoln-Douglas debates, 146–150, 156, 158, 159

Douglass, Frederick, 76–80, 133
Dred Scott decision, 137–141,
    145, 149
Dunmore, Lord, 45

electoral college, three-fifths ratio
    in the, 47, 87
Emerson, John, 137, 138, 139
Emerson, Ralph Waldo, 116
England, 13, 19
Equiano, Olaudah, 25–26

Florida, 89
    secession of, 163
Fort Johnson, S.C., 4, 11
Fort Moultrie, S.C., 4, 6
Fort Sumter, S.C., 4, 6, 7, 96, 163
Franklin, Benjamin, 129
Freeport, Ill., 146, 149
Freeport doctrine, 149–150
Free Press, 65
Free-Soiler party, 109, 125, 126–
    127, 130, 133
Frémont, John C., 137
Friends, *see* Quakers and the
    Underground Railroad
Fugitive Slave Law, 48, 100–
    103, 115–116, 120, 122–
    126, 133

Gadsden, James, 105
Gadsden Purchase, 105
Galesburg, Ill., 146
Garrison, William Lloyd, 64–
    71, 140

*Genius of Universal Emancipa-
    tion,* 66
George III, King, 43–45
Georgia, 6, 7
    secession of, 163
Ghana, 24
Gray, Thomas R., 55, 57, 59
Greene, Ann Terry, 72
Greene, Mrs. Nathanael (Cather-
    ine), 16

Hannibal, Mo., 146
Harpers Ferry, Va., raid on, 151–
    154, 159
Harth, Mingo, 54, 55
Hayne, Robert Y., 94
Henry, Prince, the Navigator, 34
Herald (Newburyport), 64

Illinois, 80, 81, 84, 85, 100, 103,
    107, 110, 125, 138, 139,
    143, 146
Indiana, 80
Indians, American:
    the Arawak, 35–36
    as first slaves in South Amer-
        ica, 35–36
indigo, 19, 41
Industrial Revolution, 20–21
Iowa, 125

Jack, Gullah, 53
Jackson, Andrew, 90, 92–97
Jacksonville, Ill., 110

James Island, S.C., 4, 11
Jamestown, Va., 36
Jamison, D. F., 3
Jefferson, Thomas, 43, 89, 129
Jonesboro, Ill., 146
Journal of the Times, 65

Kalamazoo, Mich., 136
Kansas, 108, 109, 111, 124–125, 128, 130, 133, 135, 151, 161
Kansas-Nebraska Act, 107–114, 115, 117, 119, 124–126, 128–129, 134, 145, 146
Kentucky, 80, 85, 100
Know-Nothing party, 110

Lafayette Emigration Society, 127
Lawrence, Kans., 125
  raid on, 130–131
Leavenworth, Kans., 125
Lee, Robert E., 152
Lexington and Concord, battle of, 46
Liberator, 66–68, 70
Liberia, slaves shipped to, 62–63, 113
Lincoln, Abraham:
  antislavery speeches of, 134–137, 141–142
  as candidate for Senate, 143–150
  Cooper Union speech of, 156, 158–160
  early years of, 80–81

Lincoln, Abraham (*Cont.*)
  election of, as President, 1, 155–161
  and fall of Fort Sumter, 9, 10, 96
  inauguration of, 9, 164–166
  and the Kansas-Nebraska Act, 109–114
  as a lawyer, 81–85
  and the Lincoln-Douglas debates, 146–150, 156
  in House of Representatives, 102–103, 110
Lincoln-Douglas debates, 146–150, 156
linen fabrics, 14
Louisiana:
  admission of, as a slave state, 87
  secession of, 163
Louisiana Territory, 87
Lovejoy, Elijah P., 82, 131

McClure's Magazine, 135
Maine, admission as a state of, 88
Mali, 24
Mason, James M., 101
Mason and Dixon's Line, 76, 88
Massachusetts, 14, 15, 88, 116, 117
  abolition of slavery in, 42–43, 46
Medill, Joseph, 161
Memphis, Tenn., 105
Mexican War, the, 99–100, 102

Mexico, 50, 99, 120

Mississippi, secession of, 103

Mississippi River, 46, 72, 87, 146

Missouri, 72, 88, 89, 108, 125, 126, 127, 128, 130, 137, 138, 139
  admission of, as a slave state, 88, 108

Missouri Compromise, 88–90, 104, 105, 111, 113, 115, 128, 138, 140
  repeal of, 108
  unconstitutionality of, 140

Missouri River, 88, 125

Monroe, James, 89

Monrovia, Liberia, 62

Mount Vernon, Va., 61

Mulberry Grove plantation, 16, 17, 18

Muslim traders, selling of slaves by, 24–25, 34

Nantucket, Mass., 79

National Constitutional Union party, 162

New Bedford, Mass., 79

Nebraska Territory (see also Kansas-Nebraska Act), 107, 108, 111, 124

Newburyport, Mass., 64

New England:
  abolitionists in, 64–75, 116–117, 119
  cotton mills in, 13, 19

New England (Cont.)
  slavery in, 40–43
  "triangular trade" of, 41–42, 45

New Hampshire, 104, 155

New Jersey, 120
  abolition of slavery in, 46

New Mexico Territory, 100, 101

New York, 25, 160
  abolition of slavery in, 46

New York Evening Post, 156

Niño, Pedro Alonso, 35

North, the:
  slavery in, 1, 40–43
  population of, 87

North America, first black slaves in, 36

North Carolina, 162

North Star, 79

Northwest Ordinance, ban on slavery in, 46

Northwest Territory, 46

nullification, doctrine of, 92–96

Ohio, 131, 160, 161

Ohio River, 46, 80, 88, 121

Osawatomie, Kans., 134, 151

Ottawa, Ill., 146, 148

Pacific Ocean, 35, 125

Panama, Isthmus of, 35

Pennsylvania, 99, 120
  abolition of slavery in, 46

Peru, 35

Philadelphia, Pa., 46, 164

Phillips Exeter Academy, 155
Pickens, Francis W., 7–10
Pierce, Franklin, 104, 105
plantations, overseers of, 31
political parties, realignment of, 109–110
popular sovereignty, 107, 140–141
Pottawatomie Creek, raid on, 130–131, 133, 134
Portugal, 34
Poyas, Peter, 53–55
Prosser, Gabriel, 50–52, 60

Quakers and the Underground Railroad, 121
Quincy, Ill., 146

railroad, transcontinental, 105, 107
Randolph, John, 62
Republican party, 136, 143, 148, 159, 160, 165
    formed, 109
    position on slavery, 159, 160, 161
Revolutionary War, see American Revolution
Rhode Island, abolition of slavery in, 46
rice, 19, 41
Richmond, Va., as target of a black uprising, 50, 51–52
rum, manufacture of, 41–42

Salem, Mass., 41

Sandburg, Carl, 146
Sangamon River, 80
Scott, Dred, 137–141
Scott, Winfield, 7
Sea Island, Georgia, 17
secession, 2–3, 162–163
Seward, William H., 159, 160, 161
slave(s) (see also slavery; slave trading)
    auctions, 26, 37, 40
    clothing allowance of, 30
    as field hands, 28, 29, 31
    first black, in North America, 36
    and the Fugitive Slave Law, 48, 100, 115–116, 120, 122–126, 133
    as house servants, 28–29, 53, 54
    life of, 23–33
    renting out of, 30–31
    shipping of, to Liberia, 62–63, 112
    ships, 24–26
    in South America, 35–36
    and the Underground Railroad, 120–122
    uprisings, 50–60
    workday of the, 29, 32
slavery (see also slave(s); slave trading)
    abolition of, 46, 48
    the abolitionists and, 61–75, 76–80, 130–133, 151–154

Slavery (*Cont.*)
  and the Compromise of 1850,
    48, 100–103, 115–116,
    122–124, 133
  and the Dred Scott case, 137–
    141
  effect of cotton gin on, 19–20
  as an issue in Congress, 97–
    98
  and the Kansas-Nebraska Act,
    107–109, 111–114, 115,
    124–126, 128–129
  and the Missouri Compromise,
    88–90, 105, 113, 138
  in the North, 1, 40–43
  Republican party position on,
    159, 160
  in the South, 1, 2, 13, 17, 40,
    41, 43
  as portrayed in *Uncle Tom's
    Cabin,* 118–119
  and the Wilmot Proviso, 99–
    100
slave trading:
  in the District of Columbia,
    97, 101
  New England merchants in,
    business, 41
Smith, Gerrit, 133
Songai, 24
South, the:
  effect of cotton gin on, 19–20
  population of, 87
  principal cash crops of, 19

South (*Cont.*)
  slavery in, 1, 2, 17, 37, 40, 41,
    43
South America, first slaves in,
    35–36
Southampton, Va., 55
South Carolina, 40, 129
  nullification act of, 90, 92, 93,
    94–96
  secession of, 2–4, 162–163
Southwest, the, 2, 99, 105
spirituals, Negro, 32
Springfield, Ill., 80, 82, 141,
    161, 163
Star of the West (steamer), 7,
    8
St. Louis, Mo., 88
Stowe, Harriet Beecher, 118–
    119, 126
Sullivan's Island, S.C., 4
Sumner, Charles, 128–129
Supreme Court, U.S., 145
  Dred Scott decision of, 137–
    141, 149

Taney, Roger Brooke, 138
Tappan, Arthur, 66
tariff of abominations, 90–96
Texas, 100, 125
tobacco, 19, 41
Topeka, Kansas, 125
Travis, Joseph, 57
"triangular trade," 41–42, 45
Tubman, Harriet, 122

Turner, Nat, 55–60, 61, 64, 152, 159

Uncle Tom's Cabin (Stowe), 118–119
Underground Railroad, 120–122
Utah Territory, 101

Vesey, Denmark, 52–55, 60
Virginia, 62
    raid on Harpers Ferry, 151–154
    secession of, 163
    slaves in, 37, 50, 51

War Department, U.S., 6, 8, 9, 10
Washington, Bushrod, 62
Washington, George, 45, 61–62, 129
Webster, Daniel, and the Compromise of 1850, 94–95, 100–103

West Africa:
    blacks of, 23–24, 41
    slave-raiding expeditions in, 24–25
West Indies, 24, 35, 41
Whig party, 109, 136
Whitney, Eli:
    education of, at Yale College, 15–16
    invention of cotton gin by, 13, 14, 18
Whitney, Elizabeth, 15
Whitney, Henry C., 135
Whittier, John Greenleaf, 117
Wilmot, David, 99
Wilmot Proviso, 99–100
Wisconsin Territory, 87, 138
wool fabrics, 14
Wyoming Territory, 107

Yates, Richard, 110
Yorktown, battle of, 46
Ysabel (steamer), 11

About the Author

LeRoy Hayman was born and grew up in Chicago, Illinois. He began writing in high school, where he was the coauthor of several school plays.

After receiving his master's degree from the University of Illinois, Mr. Hayman taught for several years. With the onset of World War II, he served in the Pacific as a naval officer. Following the war, Mr. Hayman turned his talents to writing and editing.

LeRoy Hayman is particularly interested in American history, and has written on many subjects in this area. Among his books are *Harry S. Truman: A Biography; Leaders of the American Revolution; O Captain: The Death of Abraham Lincoln;* and *What You Should Know About the U.S. Constitution.* The author and his wife now make their home in Great Neck, New York. They have two children.

About the Illustrator

Louis Glanzman was raised in Virginia, but moved to New York when he was thirteen. By the age of sixteen, he was writing and illustrating his own comic strip. Mr. Glanzman was in the Air Force in World War II. Later, as an observer for the Air Force during the Korean War, he traveled throughout the Far East, and on his return, he did several paintings for the Air Force Historical Society. His paintings are often in art exhibitions: some have also been on display at the White House. Now a well-known artist, he has illustrated a number of books.

Mr. Glanzman lives in Long Island with his wife and four daughters.